Atlas of Insects

Illustrated by
Tony Swift & **Adrian Williams**
Consultant **Dr. John Gray**

Maps by Geographical Projects London

Michael Tweedie
Atlas of Insects

Heinemann London

Geographical Director **Shirley Carpenter**
Editor **Geoffrey Rogers**
Art Director **Roger Hyde**
Assistant **Douglas Sneddon**

William Heinemann Ltd., 15–16 Queen Street, London, W1X 8BE
London   Melbourne   Toronto
Johannesburg   Auckland

First Published 1974
© Aldus Books Limited, London, 1974
SBN 434 79982 3
Printed and bound in Spain by Roner S.A.

Contents

Introduction

ATLAS OF INSECTS presents a fresh insight into the world of this highly successful group of animals. It describes the distribution of insects in the zoogeographical realms—the term naturalists use to describe areas of the world that have distinctive animal populations—an aspect of insect life rarely covered at this level.

The present distribution of insects around the world has been caused by a number of events, as diverse as continental drift, the effects of the Ice Age, and transportation by man. These are the themes of Chapter 1, which explains how insects of the different zoogeographical realms have arrived in their present homes. The next six chapters look in detail at some of the characteristic insects of each realm, from the brilliantly coloured butterflies of the South American rain forest to the strange, stilt-legged sand beetles of the Namib Desert in south-western Africa. Chapter 8 considers the adaptations, sometimes weird and wonderful, shown by insects that live on isolated islands. ATLAS OF INSECTS also examines the relationships—both hostile and friendly—between man and insects.

Easily identifiable symbols overlaid on full-colour relief maps show the distribution of a wide range of insects in each zoo-geographical realm. Over 80 of the insects mentioned in the text are brought to life in beautiful full-colour illustrations which, unless a note appears in the caption, show the insects at life-size.

The text is clear and non-technical, scientific names for insects being used only where no common name exists or where confusion could arise with other species. A list on page 124 shows the scientific names of the insects featured in the book.

From the opening pages, where the question "What is an insect?" is lucidly answered, to the chart of insect fossil history at the back of the book, ATLAS OF INSECTS is not only attractive to look at, but also rewarding to study.

What is an Insect?

Insects have a segmented, often rigid, outer covering and segmented or jointed limbs, and they shed the outer covering at intervals as they grow. They are, however, by no means the only animals that display these features, which are characteristic of all the members of the great division, or Phylum, of the Animal Kingdom called the Arthropoda, which includes the insects and a number of other subdivisions, or Classes, as well. Arthropods that are familiar animals, but are not insects, include spiders, scorpions, centipedes, millipedes, and crustaceans such as woodlice and crabs.

Features which distinguish the insects from the other arthropods are the division of the body into three distinct parts, head, thorax, and abdomen; the possession of three pairs of jointed legs, never more; and the frequent possession of wings. No other arthropods ever have wings.

A woodlouse. It belongs to the Class Crustacea in which the body-segments and legs are various in number and arrangement. Woodlice have seven pairs of legs.

A spider. It is a member of the Class Arachnida and the body is divided into a combined head-thorax (cephalothorax) and the abdomen is not segmented. It has four pairs of legs.

A scorpion. Also belongs to the Arachnida and has four pairs of legs and a pair of claws as well. The abdomen, which includes the slender tail, is segmented.

A centipede. A member of the Class Chilopoda. There are numerous body-segments and pairs of legs, the number being different in the various kinds of centipedes from about 20 to over 100.

An earwig. An insect that runs but seldom flies, although it has wings.

A butterfly. An insect whose chief mode of progression is by flying.

Both these have a distinct head, thorax, and abdomen, and three pairs of legs, all indications that they are true insects.

1 Insect Distribution

The natural distribution of animals about the world is determined by two wholly distinct factors. The most obvious of these is the environmental one that depends on latitude and altitude and the types of climate produced as a result of them. In general it is warm near the equator and at sea level and colder nearer the poles and higher up the mountains. Rainfall also varies in response to geographical conditions so that tropical areas may be covered by evergreen forest where abundant rain falls throughout the year, or by savannah (grassland with scattered trees) where the rain is seasonal, or may present a desert landscape of bare rock and sand where little or no rain falls. The temperate lands vary in a similar way with forest, open grassland, and cool deserts. Around both North and South poles desert also prevails, not from lack of water, which falls abundantly as snow, but because it is frozen to ice and so inaccessible to life processes.

In ascending the slopes of the high mountains the same climatic succession is encountered, from tropical forest or desert (in equatorially situated mountains like the northern Andes) through temperate conditions to a cold desert of snowfields and glaciers at great heights.

If distribution depended solely on climate we could expect faunas in similar environments at the same latitude to be closely similar all round the world, but this is far from being the case. The rain forests of Asia, Africa, and South America support very different groups of animals, and so do the steppes and pampas of Asia and South America. We explain this by supposing that evolution has proceeded independently in areas that are separated by barriers to the movement of animals, such as oceans and, less importantly, mountain ranges and deserts.

The largest insects known to have existed on the earth lived during the latest part of the Carboniferous period, about 290 million years ago, at the time when the earliest reptiles had just evolved from amphibian ancestors. These were enormous dragonflies, the largest, Meganeura monyi, *having a wing-span of 27 inches. Fossils of their huge, densely reticulated wings have been found at Commentry in France. The great swamps in which the coal-bearing strata were deposited were an ideal environment for aquatic insects.*

The truth of the continental drift theory remained in doubt for many years after it was first proposed, but it is now accepted as a fact of geology, and research during the past decade has provided a fairly clear picture of the movements involved and of their geological timing.

Up to middle Triassic times, about 210 million years ago, the lands of the world comprised a single supercontinent which has been named Pangaea. About that time a northern and southern land mass began to split apart from each other; these have received the names Laurasia and Gondwana.

By the end of the Triassic, about 195 million years ago, the split was already complete, though the two remained close or even in contact, near a position now represented by the Strait of Gibraltar. About the same time a large mass detached itself from the south-eastern part of Gondwana and began a long and amazing journey northward to its present situation as the great triangular subcontinent of India. Africa detached itself from Antarctica and moved northward, rotating a little so as to close up the ancient sea called Tethys between eastern Laurasia and Gondwana. Rather later, during the Jurassic and Cretaceous periods,

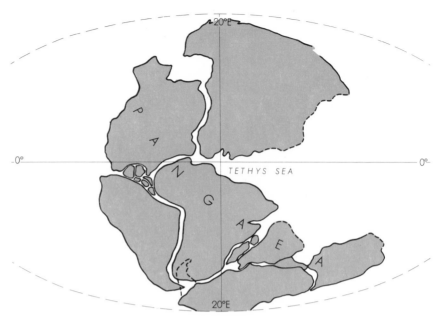

End of Permian period, about 225 million years ago.

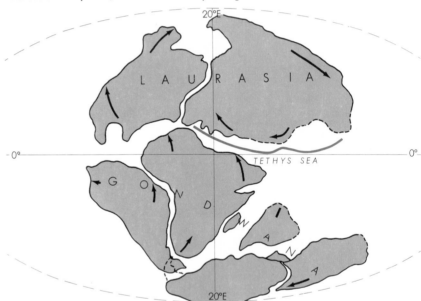

End of Triassic period, about 195 million years ago.

Different types of animals will be restricted in this way in varying degrees: those that run or crawl on the land, very effectively; dwellers in fresh waters even more so; flying animals far less.

Examination of the fossil record, and of certain aspects of present-day distribution of animals, suggest that access between the continents was easier in early geological times than it is now. At one time former "land bridges" across the oceans were postulated, which were said to have foundered and disappeared in some way that was never explained. In 1915 a German scientist, Alfred Wegener, proposed an alternative explanation. Inspired in the first place by the obvious jig-saw puzzle "fit" of the New World continents against Europe and Africa across the Atlantic Ocean, he suggested that the continents had once been joined together in a single great land mass which he called Pangaea or "All-earth." This, he believed, broke up into fragments, which then drifted apart like gigantic icebergs.

This theory of continental drift was at first rejected by orthodox

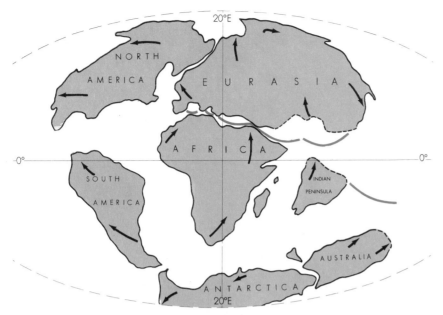

End of Cretaceous period, about 65 million years ago.

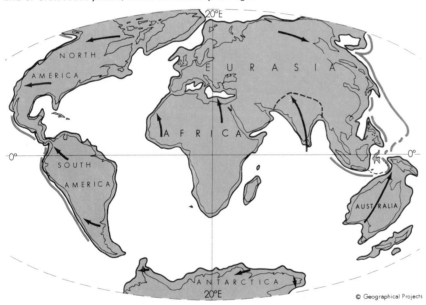

Present day.

between 195 and 65 million years ago, North and South America moved westward separately, opening up the great rift that now forms the Atlantic Ocean. All these movements have continued during the past 60 to 70 million years, the Cenozoic era The Atlantic has widened and India has completed its great northward journey, piling up against Laurasia and becoming part of what we call Asia. Along the line of this collision arose the Himalayas. About or soon after the end of the Cretaceous period, 50 to 60 million years ago, Australia became detached from Antarctica and moved northward. Of all the southern continents Antarctica has moved least.

The drifting of the continents has been shown recently to be a consequence of the even more revolutionary theory of plate tectonics. This maintains that the crust of the Earth, under both continents and oceans, is divided into a number of great plates of heavy rock, 60 miles thick, separated by seams rather like those between the shields that make up the carapace of a turtle. The 22-mile-thick continents are plateaus of lighter granitic rock embedded in the surface of the plates. The continents have preserved their outlines but the plates undergo alteration of their leading and following edges.

On these maps the solid red lines show oceanic trenches and the black arrows indicate the direction of movement of the continents since drift began.

geologists, but during the past 10 to 15 years evidence has been obtained that establishes it as a fact of geology. The break-up of Pangaea started in the late Triassic period, 200 million years ago, and began as a separation into a northern and a southern super-continent named respectively Laurasia and Gondwana. The maps show how Laurasia broke apart into Eurasia and North America and Gondwana fragmented to form Antarctica, Africa, Australia, and South America, and also peninsular India, which moved north and became joined to Laurasia.

The derivation of the mammals from the reptiles started at approximately the same time as the beginning of the drift, and by far the greater part of their evolution has taken place after the continents separated. Birds arose from reptiles later still. A glance at the table of geological periods on page 122 shows that insect evolution was already under way in the Carboniferous period, 300 million years ago, and that most of the main orders of insects were already differentiated in Triassic times. The inference is

THE ZOOGEOGRAPHICAL REGIONS OF THE WORLD

Projection: Gall

Scale: 1:46,100,000 equatorial scale

Miles

Kilometres

The Palaearctic & Nearctic regions are sometimes combined as the Holarctic region.

Palaearctic region

Nearctic region

Neotropical region

Ethiopian region

Oriental region

Australian region

Island region

Transitional zones

80°

80°

40°

ARCTIC CIRCLE

E U R O P E

A S I A

40°

TROPIC OF CANCER

A F R I C A

EQUATOR 0°

AUSTRALIA

TROPIC OF CAPRICORN

40°

ANTARCTIC CIRCLE

A N T A R C T I C A

40°

80°

120°

160°

© Geographical Projects

that they developed on Pangaea and spread all over the ancient super-continent. From this we would expect the insects to be more uniformly distributed over the continents than mammals and birds, and indeed they are so.

The primitive insects, both winged and flightless, have a world-wide distribution because they came into existence a very long time ago. The more recently evolved groups are widely spread because most of these can fly, and so have crossed the oceanic and other boundaries that divide the continents. For the same reason, of course, birds are more evenly distributed than mammals although they evolved later.

On the other hand climate has a stronger restricting influence on the distribution of insects than on that of birds and mammals because the latter, being warm-blooded, really create an artificial climate in their bodies that can be kept uniform over a wide range of surrounding temperatures. The temperature of an insect changes with its surroundings, and although some kinds are adapted to endure cold these are far fewer in number of species than those inhabiting warm climates. Some whole orders, such as the termites and stick-insects, are almost restricted to the tropics, but they are found in equatorial lands all round the world.

The science of zoogeography is concerned with the distribution of animals as determined by their origins and movements about the world in the past rather than by climate. It has been founded chiefly on vertebrate animals, especially mammals, freshwater fishes, and some of the birds, reptiles, and amphibians. It is true that insects, owing to their early origins and great mobility, are rather poor indicators in zoogeography, but this is only relatively so, and we shall consider them in the context of the zoogeographical regions, or realms, devoting a chapter to each one of these, and the last chapter to the particular characteristics of insects that inhabit islands.

The name Grylloblatta *implies affinity with both crickets and cockroaches, and the rare and obscure insects of this genus are regarded as surviving relicts of an ancient group ancestral to these two orders. They inhabit localities high in the mountains of North America, Siberia, and Japan, and are usually found under stones near glaciers. The American species* Grylloblatta campodeiformis *is shown here greatly enlarged.*

The formation of the regions has to be considered in terms of their ancient geology, that is their relation to the very long, slow course of continental drift, and also in terms of climate and recent geological events such as changes of land and sea level.

The Palaearctic region (Europe and northern Asia) has its origin in the larger of the two pieces into which Laurasia was divided by the Atlantic rift, the smaller being the Nearctic region (North America). Biological evidence of this ancient association, combined with the long period of early separation from the components of Gondwana, is scanty, but one very curious and primitive group of flightless insects seems to be of Laurasian origin. This is the order Grylloblattodea; the name means "cricket-cockroach," and some features of these two groups are combined, suggesting that the insects are living remnants of the ancient stock from which the Orthoptera (crickets and grasshoppers) and the Dictyoptera (cockroaches and mantises) were derived. Only six species of the whole order are known, and they inhabit high, cold localities near the edge of glaciers in North America, Russia, and Japan. They are blind and live under stones, and have probably survived the competition of more advanced insects by becoming adapted to an environment where few insects are found. The North American *Grylloblatta campodeiformis* is the best known species.

The more recent geological history of the Palaearctic and Nearctic regions suggests that access from one to the other has in the past been more easy than it is today. This is because the Bering Strait has been closed for long periods providing a true

The Camberwell beauty butterfly is called mourning cloak in America, a translation of the German name Trauermantel. *It has a very wide distribution in the Northern Hemisphere, being found from western Europe to Japan and also in temperate North America. It does not thrive in Britain, and is only a rare visitor.*

land bridge, and the climate preceding the Ice Age, in which we are still living, was much less severe than now, enabling animals of the temperate zones to range farther north. The Apollo butterflies, found on mountains all over the Palaearctic region, occur on the Rockies in North America but not on any mountains east of them. Other familiar butterflies, such as the mourning cloak, or Camberwell beauty, are common to the two regions, and many genera are represented in both regions by closely similar species. Some zoogeographers unite the two regions under the name Holarctic.

The Oriental region (southern Asia) is bounded to the north, and separated from the Palaearctic region, by the great Himalayan mountains that rose out of the Tethys sea when peninsular India collided with Laurasia after its long drift northwards from Gondwana. Although it has long been joined to the northern and separated from the southern land masses, it must not be forgotten that the region is of Gondwana origin.

The Ethiopian region (Africa south of the Sahara) is a relic of Gondwana, but was never far from Laurasia and became joined to it rather early in the history of continental drift. It is now isolated from the Palaearctic and Oriental regions by deserts and narrow seas, but there have been periods in fairly recent geological times when access to it from the lands to the north and east was easier than at the present time. Its closest affinity is with the Oriental region.

The bugs of the family Peloridiidae *are minute and obscure insects, of a primitive type, which are found in wet moss in southern America, southern Australia, and New Zealand. Their distribution is of interest as it supports the theory that South America, Antarctica, and Australia once formed a continuous land mass, since broken up by continental drift. The species* Peloridium hammoniorum *is shown here at about 40 times actual size.*

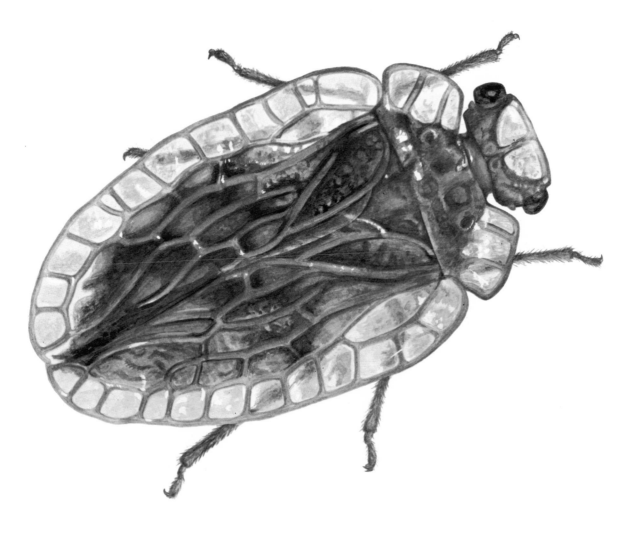

The Neotropical region (South America) was separated from the Nearctic region for a very long period after its breakaway from Africa. The separation was not in the region of the Panama isthmus but farther north, so that the Central American region is made up of the northern part of a formerly isolated South America. During the Cenozoic period (from 65 million years ago to the present-time) some migration of tree-living animals took place, probably on floating rafts of vegetation carried between islands that arose between the two continents. At some time in the Pliocene epoch (7 million to 2 million years ago) a land connection rose out of the sea and a horde of Nearctic mammals moved southward, almost exterminating the isolated and highly peculiar mammal fauna of the old Neotropical island continent. Stone-age man later continued this process and modern man appears to be completing it.

The Neotropical insects, however, held their own and some of them, such as the io moth, invaded the northern continent. The South American insect fauna thus remained inviolate and is in fact as distinct from that of the rest of the world as the Australian.

Australia, including the northern part of its continental shelf on which New Guinea stands, was detached from Antarctica late in the history of continental drift, only 50 or 60 million years ago. It performed a northward journey almost as long as that of India and reached a position south-east of the Oriental part of Asia, but the two regions were never joined by continuous land. The unique Australian mammal fauna did not therefore suffer the same fate as that of the Neotropical region, though it is now being destroyed much more rapidly than was that of ancient South America. A complex chain of islands between the Oriental and Australian regions has made the passage of winged insects fairly easy in both directions and much interchange of insect faunas has taken place.

Antarctica is now almost uninhabitable for insects, but it once enjoyed a milder climate and at the beginning of the break-up of Gondwana formed a bridge between Australia and South America. A family of primitive bugs, the Peloridiidae, bears witness to the reality of the ancient southern continent. They are flightless and live in wet moss and so are not easily dispersed by natural causes. Six species live in Chile and Patagonia, five in Tasmania and southern Australia, six in New Zealand, and two in Lord Howe Island (between Australia and New Zealand). Fossils closely resembling them, and of Triassic age, bear out this interpretation of their distribution.

Another sort of distribution of an ancient type of insect is that of the Petalurid dragonflies. These were the dominant dragonflies in the Jurassic period, which followed the Triassic and saw the heyday of the dinosaurs. Being insects of powerful flight they ranged over the ancient world, the derivatives of Laurasia and Gondwana alike. Now they are found in a few widely scattered localities of limited extent. Nine living species are known, over half of which live in Australia and New Zealand, but the others are found as small separate remnants in Chile, eastern and western North America, and Japan.

Since man took to living in houses and sailing the seas he has

done much to promote the spread of many insect species, and some of these now live mainly in close association with him. The domestic cockroaches and the house cricket are obvious cases of this, as is the silverfish, which is unknown in the wild state and lives in human dwellings all over the world. It was doing so over 2,000 years ago, for it is recognizably described in a Chinese dictionary compiled between 400 and 200 B.C.

The transportation of insects has led to many of them assuming the status of pests, especially when they feed on some widely grown crop, and several instances of this are described in the following chapters.

A peculiar and interesting instance of the spread through human agency of a harmless insect is that of the monarch, or milkweed, butterfly. A native of America, it has extended its range in a little over a century to Hawaii, Australia, New Zealand, and many islands in the Pacific Ocean and the Malay Archipelago, and across the Atlantic Ocean to the Canary Islands. It seems that this spread is due to the introduction of the milkweed plants on which its larva feeds combined with its own tendency to far-ranging migration. The butterfly can be welcomed wherever it goes as it is a beautiful insect and also helps to control the introduced milkweeds, which often become noxious weeds.

The little silverfish, shown here greatly magnified, is a familiar inhabitant of kitchen cupboards all over the world. In this environment it does little harm, but it may damage books and papers that are seldom used or handled. It is a purely domestic insect, unknown in any habitat in the open, and has probably lived in human dwellings for several thousand years. It is also of interest as an example of a very primitive type of wingless insect.

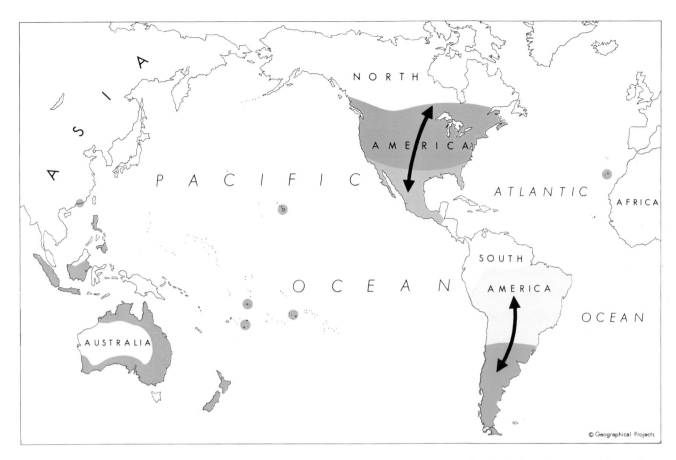

The North American monarch butterfly not only migrates seasonally in its home continent, but it also undertakes dispersal flights over the oceans and has become widely established. In South America a closely allied subspecies migrates seasonally but has not dispersed beyond the continent.

The monarch, or milkweed, is one of the world's most famous butterflies. It is a native of North America, but has spread widely over the world in recent times, probably as a result of the dispersal by man of the milkweeds that are its food plant. Its strong instinct to migrate has helped to promote this spread. In North America its annual migrations have been closely studied and individual butterflies have been shown, by marking and recapture, to have flown up to 2,000 miles.

2 The Palaearctic Region

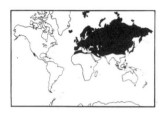

Europe, Africa north of
the Sahara Desert, Asia Minor,
the Middle East, Iran,
Afghanistan, USSR, Mongolia,
northern China, Korea,
and Japan.

The greater part of this region comprises the temperate lands of Eurasia, extending over a huge area from western Europe to eastern Asia, with the islands of Britain and Japan as its western and eastern outliers. The insect fauna of this area is remarkably uniform: Japan and Britain have 23 species of butterflies in common, which extend more or less continuously across the vast intervening territory.

The gipsy moth, formerly found in the East Anglian fens, but now extinct in Britain, is common all over Europe northward to Denmark and south Sweden, and its range extends without a break eastward to the eastern U.S.S.R., Manchuria, and Japan. Britain is really very fortunate to be without the gipsy moth, for wherever it is abundant its larvae cause devastation by devouring the leaves of orchard and woodland trees. It is a curious insect in several respects. The male and female are wholly different in appearance, the male being mainly dark brown and the larger female being white with some faint darker markings. Although its wings are fully developed, the female does not fly and lays its eggs near the pupal cocoon. In view of this, it is hard to see how the moth manages to disperse itself in the regions where it occurs, though it certainly does so, often with disastrous effects. The males are strong fliers, but this can have no effect on the dispersal of future generations of the species. How, then, does the gipsy moth spread? It has been found that the very young caterpillars, which are covered with long, fine hairs, readily become wind-borne like thistle-down or gossamer spiders. Unlike many moth and butterfly larvae they are not particular about what leaves they eat—almost any tree or shrub will do—so wherever they happen to land they are likely to find plenty of food.

The swallowtail butterfly extends from western Europe through temperate Asia to Sakhalin Island and Japan, but it has a discontinuous distribution, being absent from large areas in central Asia. It is also found in subarctic and western North America, where it is known as the Old World swallowtail. The British subspecies lives in marshes, but in Europe it flies in open country up to 6,000 feet in the mountains.

The green lestes damselfly also ranges right across the Palaearctic region, but with a distinctly more northern distribution and less frequent penetration into the subtropics than the gipsy moth. Like all the dragonflies and damselflies, it passes its early stages in fresh water, usually in a thick growth of reeds and rushes. Almost any sort of still waters seem to suit it, from acid peat water on moors to brackish water near the sea, and this tolerance of habitat probably accounts in part for its wide distribution.

The swallowtail butterfly displays a Palaearctic distribution of a different type: it occurs in Britain and the whole of Europe eastward to Japan, but by no means continuously. In central Asia it extends from an area north-west of the Himalayas eastward to the Pacific coast of China. To the north, isolated populations of the swallowtail are found around Lake Balkhash and Lake Baikal; in the extreme south-eastern part of the U.S.S.R. and the adjoining part of Manchuria; and in the Kamchatka Peninsula. It also inhabits the offshore island of Sakhalin and Japan. Finally there is a small outlying colony in southern Arabia, which represents its only penetration into the tropics. Every one of these isolated populations consists of a distinct sub-species. Even the tiny and precarious population in the Norfolk Broads of Britain is recognizably distinct and has been named *Papilio machaon britannicus*. It differs from the subspecies found in France in having wings of a deeper yellow ground colour; also the dark markings on the wings are broader and of a deeper black. It has a quite distinct habitat preference. The French swallowtail is found on open, hilly country, such as chalk downs, but the British subspecies lives only in marshy surroundings and its larva feeds on milk-parsley, which grows in marshes. It seems likely that the British swallowtail is a relict of a race that lived during and shortly after the Ice Age in a large area of lowlands and swamps now covered by the North Sea.

The common cockchafer, or maybug, has a far more limited

The male and female gipsy moth are so different that they look like distinct species; the female is larger and lighter in colour. The moth is distributed right across Europe and Asia and has been accidentally introduced into North America. Its caterpillars feed on the leaves of various trees and often do serious damage.

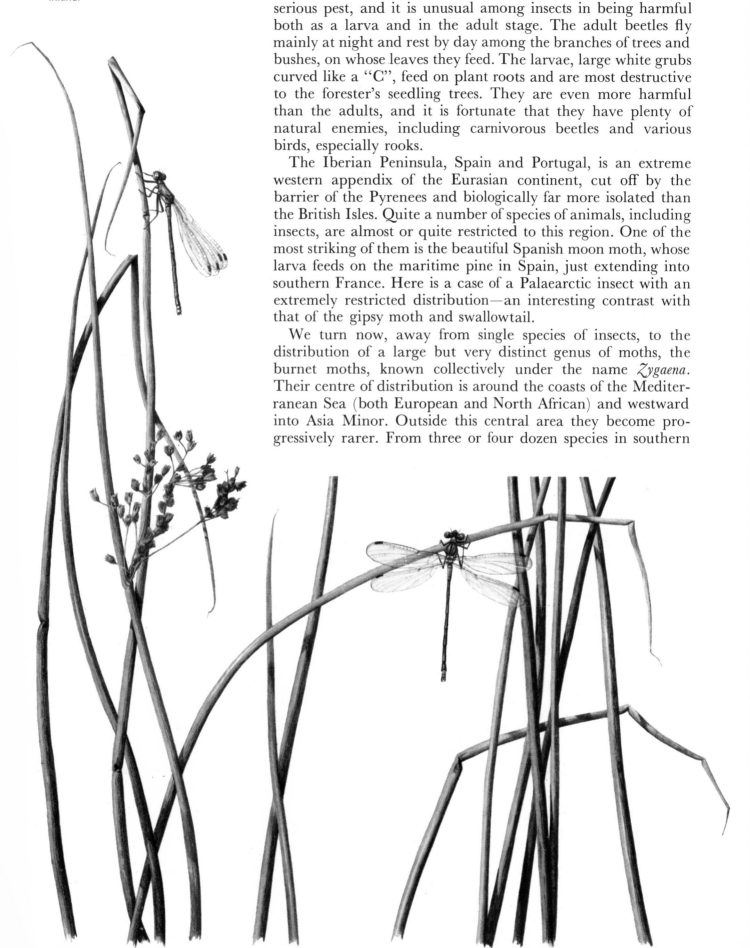

distribution. It is abundant in Britain and extends eastward on the Continent only to the area north of the Black Sea. It is absent from Spain, Greece, and most of Italy, and also from Norway and Sweden. Where this large beetle occurs it may be a serious pest, and it is unusual among insects in being harmful both as a larva and in the adult stage. The adult beetles fly mainly at night and rest by day among the branches of trees and bushes, on whose leaves they feed. The larvae, large white grubs curved like a "C", feed on plant roots and are most destructive to the forester's seedling trees. They are even more harmful than the adults, and it is fortunate that they have plenty of natural enemies, including carnivorous beetles and various birds, especially rooks.

The Iberian Peninsula, Spain and Portugal, is an extreme western appendix of the Eurasian continent, cut off by the barrier of the Pyrenees and biologically far more isolated than the British Isles. Quite a number of species of animals, including insects, are almost or quite restricted to this region. One of the most striking of them is the beautiful Spanish moon moth, whose larva feeds on the maritime pine in Spain, just extending into southern France. Here is a case of a Palaearctic insect with an extremely restricted distribution—an interesting contrast with that of the gipsy moth and swallowtail.

We turn now, away from single species of insects, to the distribution of a large but very distinct genus of moths, the burnet moths, known collectively under the name *Zygaena*. Their centre of distribution is around the coasts of the Mediterranean Sea (both European and North African) and westward into Asia Minor. Outside this central area they become progressively rarer. From three or four dozen species in southern

PALAEARCTIC REGION
(North Asia)

© Geographical Projects

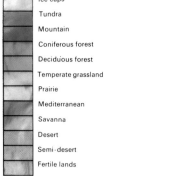

Ice caps
Tundra
Mountain
Coniferous forest
Deciduous forest
Temperate grassland
Prairie
Mediterranean
Savanna
Desert
Semi-desert
Fertile lands

Projection: Lambert's Azimuthal Equal Area

Scale: 1:21,600,000

Miles
0   100   200   300   400   500   600   700

Kilometres
0 100 200 300 400 500 600 700 800 900 1000 1100

 Alpine grizzled skipper

 House cricket

 Arctic grayling butterfly

 Japanese beetle

 Cockchafer beetle

 Plain tiger butterfly

 Desert locust

 Sacred scarab beetle

 Dewey ringlet butterfly

 Six-spot burnet moth

 Gipsy moth

 Swallowtail butterfly

 Green lestes damselfly

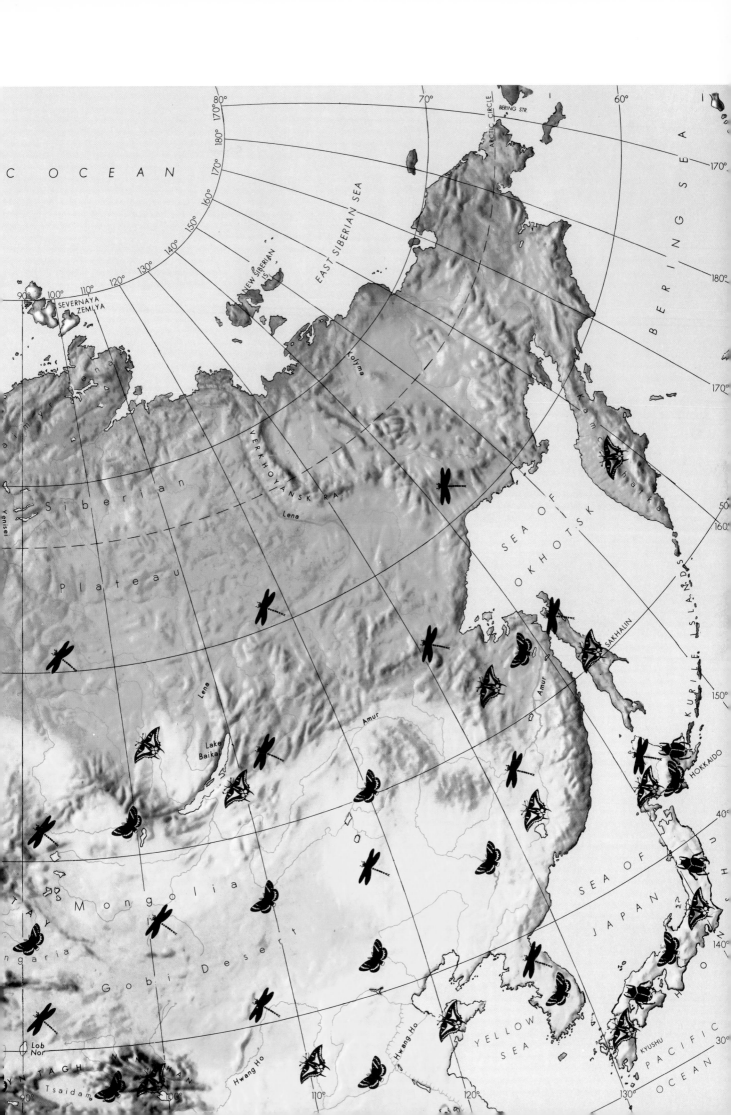

Europe the number drops to seven in Denmark and Britain and only two in the subarctic regions. Only one species extends as far as eastern Asia and Japan. There are a few species in south and east Africa, whose evolutionary ancestors seem to have strayed away from the centre of distribution in the south-western Palaearctic.

All the burnets are brightly coloured moths that fly slowly about in sunlit flowery meadows. They are not preyed upon by birds because their bodies contain an offensive, poisonous fluid. Once a bird has pecked a burnet it will avoid them thereafter, recognizing them by their conspicuous coloration, which thus serves as a warning.

The common cockchafer is often called the maybug because it is active in May and early June. It is one of the larger species of a group of beetles in which the antennae have peculiar fan-like clubs most highly developed in the males. They are organs of smell, and this formation probably gives them a larger area with which to gather molecules of scent carried on the air. The beetle is herbivorous in all its stages and does a great deal of harm to vegetation. The larvae feed on roots and the adults on the leaves of trees and bushes.

The northern polar regions and the higher slopes of mountains provide similar environments for insect life. Usually there are far fewer species there than are found in the lowlands, but arctic and alpine insects may be very numerous in terms of individuals. In the arctic tundra, the treeless region south of the polar ice, swarms of a few species of mosquitoes and black-flies emerge in summer, and people have to wear protective clothing, even hoods and veils covering the head, to keep off the millions of bloodsucking insects.

Insects of mountains and far northern environments are usually adapted for life in rigorous conditions. Frequently they are small and dark coloured, both these qualities enabling them to absorb heat rapidly when the sun shines. A small body has a larger surface area relative to its mass than a large one composed of the same substance. (If you wish to test this, peel an equal weight of large potatoes and of small ones; the small ones will take longer because they have a larger total area of peel.) When exposed to heat, the small body will therefore warm up more quickly than the large one. Also black or dark surfaces absorb radiant heat more readily than light ones, which reflect it. A black stone exposed to strong sunlight gets hot while a light-

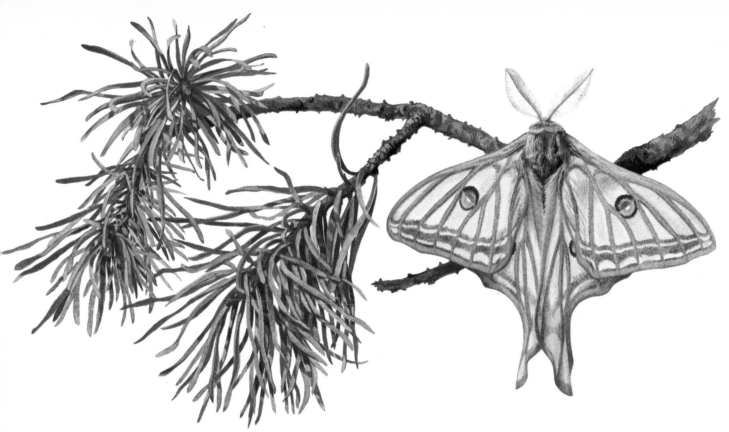

The beautiful Spanish moon moth is one of a number of insect species almost or quite confined to Spain and emphasizes the isolation of the Iberian Peninsula from the rest of Europe. Its larva feeds on pine.

The bright colours of the burnet moths serve to advertise their poisonous nature and to warn birds against trying to eat them. Two individuals of the six-spot burnet (right) and one of the southern European Provence burnet are shown here.

coloured one remains quite cool. Arctic and alpine insects come out and sit or fly about in sunshine, but hide away as soon as the sun is obscured or sets. In this way they collect and conserve as much body heat as possible.

There are many examples of dark-coloured northern and mountain insects. Among butterflies almost all the numerous species of mountain ringlet are dark brown or blackish, and the purely northern arctic grayling is brown. Some of the species of mountain ringlet are found at low altitudes in the far north, but almost all of the beautiful Apollo butterflies inhabit mountain ranges. The subspecies shown on page 31 is confined to the

European Alps, but the centre of distribution of the Apollos is the Tibetan massif. The species found there at great heights are, as one would expect, darker in colour than those of lower altitudes.

The resemblances between northern and alpine insects seem generally to be the result of convergent evolution, which has produced similar characteristics in response to similar environments. The matter goes further than this, however, for identical species of butterflies, moths, and many other insects are found in the far north and also on mountains far to the south, separated from the arctic populations by hundreds of miles of lowland country in which they are wholly absent. Convergent evolution can produce similarities, but the same species cannot possibly arise independently in widely separated localities. There must be another explanation for this distribution.

To understand how this has come about we must look at the recent geological history of the northern temperate lands. Remember that in the context of geology "recent" implies anything up to one or two million years ago. During the past million years or so the Earth has passed through a number of periods, four or five at least, of abnormally cold climate, alternating with periods in which the climate was warmer. These are known respectively as glacial and interglacial periods, and the whole time during which they occurred is often referred to as the Ice Age.

With the onset of a glacial period the snowline gradually advanced down the mountain sides, glaciers became established on mountains where they are normally (i.e. interglacially)

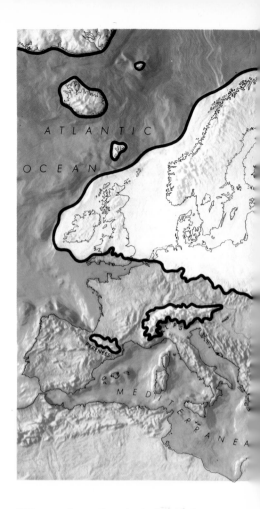

This map shows the extent of glaciation in Europe during the Ice Age. Many of the cold-loving insects that moved southwards during the glacial periods became isolated on mountains as the ice retreated.

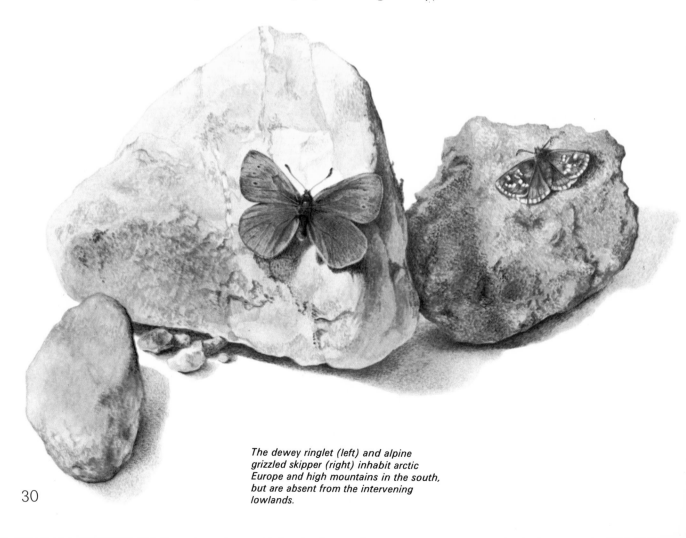

The dewey ringlet (left) and alpine grizzled skipper (right) inhabit arctic Europe and high mountains in the south, but are absent from the intervening lowlands.

30

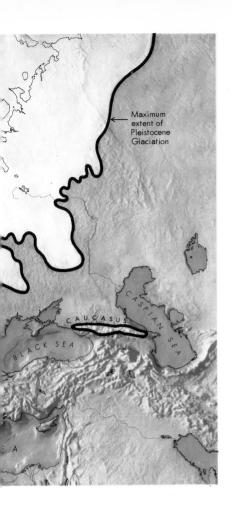

Maximum
extent of
Pleistocene
Glaciation

CAUCASUS

CASPIAN SEA

BLACK SEA

absent, and existing glaciers enlarged and advanced into the lowlands. In northern areas, such as north Britain, Scandinavia, and Canada, continuous ice-sheets formed, like those that cover Greenland and Antarctica today. Farther south ice covered the mountain ranges and skirts of ice extended from their foothills into the lowlands. All ice-free areas in what are now temperate regions became extremely cold.

Animal life of all kinds retreated before the ice. Warmth-loving species took refuge in the tropics and subtropics, while those accustomed to cold conditions moved southwards and, in mountainous regions, downwards. In this way most of Europe between the Alps and the Arctic of the present day became occupied by a uniform cold-climate fauna.

With the approach of an interglacial period this process went into reverse. The glaciers and ice-sheets dwindled and retreated. Warmth-loving insects and other animals invaded the lowlands from the south and those conditioned to the cold retreated before them. Those in the northern lowlands merely went farther north. Those around the southern mountains had an easier avenue of escape from the warmth: they ascended higher and higher up the mountain slopes. In this way, during an interglacial period (which is almost certainly what we are now in) the southern populations of cold-loving insects survive on "islands" of cold far from the northern ice and snow.

Just over 10,000 years has elapsed since the last retreat of the ice. This is too short a time for any considerable degree of evolutionary change, and so the descendants of the European lowland glacial insects and other animals (and plants as well)

This subspecies of the small Apollo butterfly is confined to the European Alps. Over the whole of their range the Apollos are mountain butterflies.

An adult and two young of the desert locust. The adult and larger of the young locusts are in the gregarious phase and so brightly coloured. This appearance is brought about by close crowding and consequent high level of activity, which in turn leads to swarm formation. The smallest young locust is in the solitary phase and will spend its life as a grasshopper does, mating but meeting few or no other individuals of its own species, and will maintain a dull green or brown coloration.

remain almost identical in their widely separated refuges in the north and in the high Alps, Pyrenees, Carpathian, and Balkan mountains. Such slight differences as have developed between the various isolated populations are recognized by regarding them as subspecies.

This "Boreo-alpine" distribution (*Boreas* was the North Wind in Greek mythology) is well shown by several European butterflies. One of these is the dewy ringlet, which flies at sea level in north and west Scandinavia and at quite high levels in the Pyrenees, the Alps, and some of the other south European ranges. The alpine grizzled skipper has a similar distribution.

We turn now from the mountain heights and arctic wastes of the Palaearctic region to its southern limits around the Mediterranean coasts of Europe and Africa and the lands of south-western Asia. The climate of this region is mostly warm and dry and the insect fauna is very different from that of the temperate and cold areas to the north.

Certainly the most notorious insect of this area is the desert locust. This is the species that is recorded in the Book of Exodus as having plagued the land of Egypt at the time when its ruler refused to permit emigration of the Jewish tribes. At irregular intervals of time locusts have always descended upon the fertile lands of the Near and Middle East and laid them waste. The desert locust is not the only species involved, but it is the most formidable and difficult to control of all of them. Its range extends well beyond the southern Palaearctic southward into Africa and eastward into the Oriental region.

Like other locusts, it is just a large grasshopper that may be encountered in small numbers at any time in the less arid parts of its range. From time to time favourable conditions cause its numbers to increase here and there over a fairly wide area, and small, relatively harmless swarms of flying locusts appear, which are carried along by the prevailing winds. If these are blowing as part of a cyclone, or atmospheric depression, the locusts are carried by the spiralling winds to the low-pressure centre of the system, where they assemble in great numbers to lay their eggs in the ground.

But such low-pressure centres are well known as areas where rain is likely to fall, and rain will promote rapid temporary growth of vegetation in desert and semi-desert regions. By following the weather in this way the locusts therefore locate and take advantage of perfect breeding grounds for their offspring, which appear in huge numbers and form the centres in which the dangerous migrating swarms originate. It has been estimated that the total weight of insects in a large locust swarm may be about 15,000 tons.

This mode of location of outbreak areas is quite different from that seen in the other kinds of "plague" locusts, which we shall consider when describing the insects of the Ethiopian region. It is the difficulty of predicting the exact areas where swarms may originate that makes the desert locust so hard to control.

A feature that all the swarming locusts have in common is the

The sacred scarab is one of the best known of all beetles. Its curious habits attracted the attention of the people of ancient Egypt and they came to regard it as sacred and made replicas of it in stone and pottery. Many of these have been found by archaeologists. It is shown here pushing a large ball of dung that it has gathered, possibly with the help of another beetle, to be buried in the soil and used for food. The beetles feed on the dung themselves and also bury stores of it to provide food for their larvae.

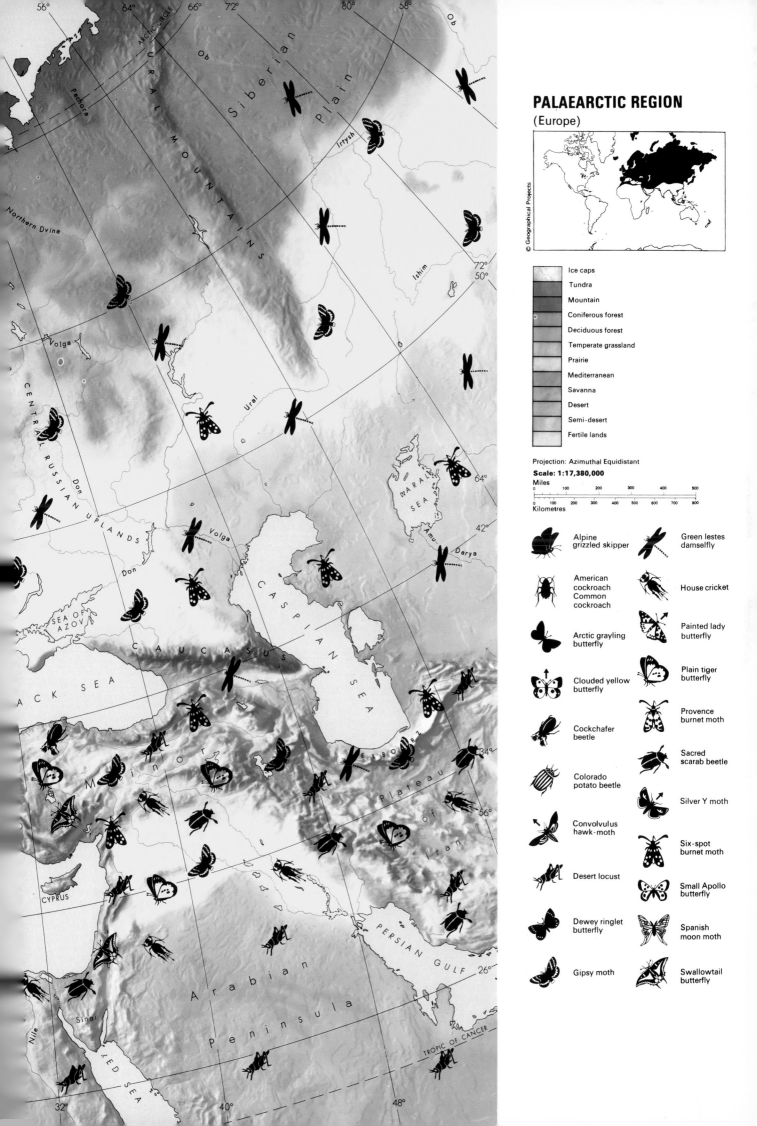

PALAEARCTIC REGION
(Europe)

© Geographical Projects

Ice caps
Tundra
Mountain
Coniferous forest
Deciduous forest
Temperate grassland
Prairie
Mediterranean
Savanna
Desert
Semi-desert
Fertile lands

Projection: Azimuthal Equidistant
Scale: 1:17,380,000
Miles
0   100   200   300   400   500
0   100 200 300 400 500 600 700 800
Kilometres

Alpine grizzled skipper

American cockroach Common cockroach

Arctic grayling butterfly

Clouded yellow butterfly

Cockchafer beetle

Colorado potato beetle

Convolvulus hawk-moth

Desert locust

Dewey ringlet butterfly

Gipsy moth

Green lestes damselfly

House cricket

Painted lady butterfly

Plain tiger butterfly

Provence burnet moth

Sacred scarab beetle

Silver Y moth

Six-spot burnet moth

Small Apollo butterfly

Spanish moon moth

Swallowtail butterfly

appearance among them of two distinct "phases," the solitary and the gregarious phase. When the insects are living a more or less blameless existence as grasshoppers, the flightless young—or "hoppers" as they are called—are brown or green and lead solitary lives. This is the solitary phase. When large numbers are crowded together, as in the outbreak centres, their appearance and behaviour change. They become brightly coloured and tend to assemble in crowds. This is the gregarious phase. More will be said on this subject when we deal with the locusts of tropical and southern Africa.

It is a relief to turn now to a useful and attractive insect, the sacred scarab beetle, which is found along the southern part of the Palaearctic region and just penetrates the Oriental region in north-western India. This beetle, itself a little over an inch long, makes a ball of cattle or goat's dung as big as a man's fist and rolls it along the ground, pushing it backwards with its hinder legs. Sometimes two beetles, of the same or different sex, share the labour of trundling the ball. When a suitable place is found, the ball is buried and the beetle or beetles stay with it underground and feed on it until it is finished. Then another ball is collected, rolled, and consumed in the same way. The beetles live in this fashion for several months, but towards the end of the summer they team up in pairs, male and female. Each pair buries a ball of dung, but in this case they prepare an underground chamber for it and the female then shreds it up and remoulds it in the shape of a pear. In the narrow neck she makes a small cavity in which she lays a single egg. Then the pair of scarabs leave it, filling in the tunnel which they have

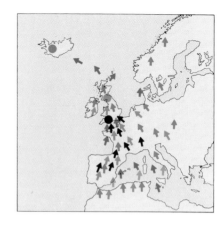

Butterfly migration in Europe. Painted lady (red arrows), clouded yellow (blue), Bath white (black).

Narrow seas such as the English Channel are no obstacle to insects with powerful flight and the instinct to migrate. The three butterflies shown here belong to species that are seen in the British Isles in the summer, but which cannot overwinter there at any stage in their life cycles. The clouded yellow (left) is recorded in Britain in most years but is only occasionally seen in large numbers. The painted lady (centre) flies north in greater or lesser numbers each year. The Bath white (right) is only recorded in Britain and northern Europe intermittently, but there have been years in which a fair number were seen. All three species have their true home in southern Europe and North Africa.

Moths as well as butterflies migrate regularly to northern Europe from the south and often cross the English Channel. As they fly at night their passage is mainly unseen, but some species come in large numbers. The big, powerful convolvulus hawk-moth (left) is a regular migrant and by no means rare. The handsome bedstraw hawk-moth (bottom right) arrives in far fewer numbers and is considered a prize by collectors in Britain. On the other hand the much smaller silver Y moth (top right) migrates in huge swarms. Large numbers of this insect may be seen feeding at flowers in late summer, during the day as well as at night.

Moth migration in Europe. Convolvulus hawk-moth (red arrows), bedstraw hawk-moth (blue), silver Y moth (black).

made, and repeat the process elsewhere. The egg hatches in due course and the larva lives on the store of food, completing its transformations in the earthen chamber and emerging as a beetle in the following spring.

The ancient Egyptians saw in the beetle's activities a symbol of the working of the universe, as they pictured it, with the ball of dung representing the earth rolling from sunrise to sunset. The scarab was therefore revered as a sacred insect and images of it in stone and pottery are frequent among archaeological relics of the period. The beetles are, of course, performing a useful service by burying the dung and blending it with the soil. Very likely the highly civilized early Egyptians appreciated this, though only their mystical beliefs about the industrious and amusing scarabs received artistic expression.

Most insects (locusts are an exception) tend to remain and breed in the vicinity where they themselves hatched from the egg, though winged species may be widely dispersed by the wind. Quite a number of Palaearctic insects, however, are known to perform seasonal migrations, rather like the well-known migrations of birds, except that most of the insects appear to fly only northwards in the spring and summer without any southward return when winter approaches.

The best observed migrations are those between the Mediterranean region and northern Europe. A number of familiar butterflies and moths (and others that are rarer and less familiar)

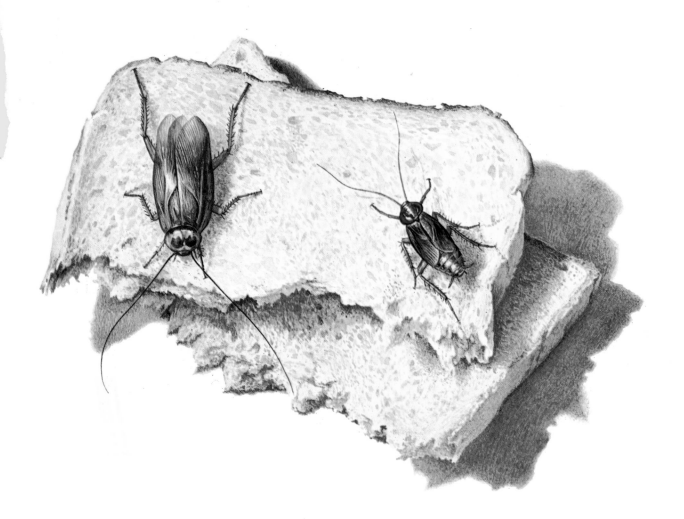

cannot live through the winter in the latitude of Britain, Holland, and Denmark in any of their stages. They breed and multiply in north Africa and southern Europe and, from some compulsion that remains unexplained, some of them fly northward in the early summer. The red admiral is one of Britain's most familiar butterflies, but all those seen there in late summer are the offspring of parents that flew across the English Channel earlier in the year. There is some evidence that these autumn butterflies fly south again, but we do not know whether they ever reach the regions where they can survive and breed during the winter.

The most celebrated migrant of all is the painted lady. Great swarms of them have been seen taking off from their breeding grounds in the African semidesert and flying away northward; they are not known to return. This butterfly is such a compulsive migrant that it has spread to all continents except Antarctica, and it is frequently seen within the Arctic Circle. The clouded yellow and Bath white butterflies behave in a similar fashion, but only fly north in numbers at intervals of many years. Both species arrived in large numbers in England in 1947, but the Bath white has hardly been seen since, though a few clouded yellows are recorded every year.

The silver Y moth has the same status as the red admiral, but it both migrates and breeds in huge numbers. People who operate illuminated moth traps in England sometimes capture hundreds of them in a single night. Some of the big hawk-moths, which fly as powerfully as birds, also migrate northward.

Two of the several kinds of cockroaches that live in human dwellings are shown here. The smaller common cockroach is the most abundant species in temperate climates such as that of northern Europe. The much larger so-called American cockroach occurs only in seaport towns in these latitudes, but is common everywhere in the tropics and subtropics. Both species are probably natives of North Africa, where they are found in the open, but they live "indoors" all round the world, carried by shipping and other forms of transport.

The convolvulus hawk-moth is one of these and appears in small numbers in late summer all over northern Europe. The beautiful bedstraw hawk-moth is always a rarity and years may go by without its being seen in northern Europe. The migrating females of these hawk-moths lay eggs in the north and the caterpillars may be found and bred through to the adult stage with the aid of artificial heat, but in the wild they are all doomed to die during the winter.

In the cold temperate parts of the world man creates for himself, in his dwellings and places of work and amusement, a climate that can be compared in quality with that of the dry subtropics. Some subtropical insects have taken advantage of this, the most important and notorious of them being the various "domestic" cockroaches. They include the common or oriental cockroach, the American cockroach, the Australian cockroach, and the German cockroach. Their names suggest homelands in widely separated parts of the world, but every one of these is based on the ill-informed guess of some early zoologist. All four are almost certainly natives of north Africa. They invaded ships in Mediterranean ports and were carried to cities and towns all over Europe and Asia in early historical times, crossing to the New World as soon as transatlantic shipping developed.

The little singing house cricket lives in the open in the same region and in western Asia, and no doubt has a similar history as a domestic insect. It is less able to cope with modern measures directed against insects than are the tough, aggressive cockroaches and has become rare. This is a pity, for it is a pleasant little creature and not really harmful. If anyone has a good word to say for cockroaches he (or she) must be an insect lover indeed.

The house cricket is a "domestic" insect, like the cockroaches, but is far less harmful and offensive. At one time it was welcome in houses on account of its cheerful chirping song, but modern obsession with hygiene has banished it from dwellings associated with a high standard of living. It has, however, found a refuge in large municipal rubbish dumps, where decay and slow burning maintain constant warm conditions. Its original home is in North Africa and western Asia.

3 The Nearctic Region

Greenland, Canada, the United States (including Alaska and the Aleutian Islands, but not Hawaii), and the desert and semi-desert area of Mexico as far south as the Tropic of Cancer.

This region comprises the North American continent from Alaska in the north to Mexico in the south, and the islands to the north-east of it, including Greenland. Climatically it is the counterpart of the Palaearctic, and the fauna of the two regions, including the insects, is very similar. The reasons for this similarity, despite the apparently effective isolation of the two regions from each other, are discussed in the first chapter.

Many of the insects of the far north are circumpolar, but the Arctic tussock moths (Genus *Gynaephora*) are characteristic of the Nearctic region, there being one species in Alaska and Canada and another in Greenland. The former, Ross's arctic tussock, is known to require four or five years to complete its life-cycle. This is an extreme case of a tendency that is often found among insects of very cold climates.

Seven species of crickets live in North America belonging to the genus *Gryllus*. These are closely allied to the common field cricket of Europe and temperate Asia. The seven American ones are so alike that until quite recently they were thought to belong to one variable species. They were identified, not by reference to preserved material in collections, but by study of their habits and distribution.

The first suspicion of complications came when an entomologist in North Carolina recognized four distinct cricket songs and found that the singers lived in different types of habitat. Further search over a wider area revealed the three additional species. Almost all of them have quite different songs. They tend to inhabit different types of country; the northern wood-cricket, for instance, lives in oak-hickory forest, others in grassland, and one, the sand field-cricket, is coastal. Their life histories differ. Some overwinter as juveniles, mature in the spring and die soon

The periodical cicada has long been famous for its appearance in swarms at intervals of several years, which correspond with the underground life of the wingless larva. These intervals are of either 13 or 17 years, and it has now been shown that not one species is involved, but six, three with the 13-year- and three with the 17-year life cycle. All six are closely similar in appearance but they never interbreed.

after, while others overwinter as eggs and only come to maturity in late summer. Finally, their geographical ranges differ, though in most cases they overlap. The different species are reluctant to hybridize in captivity.

Species arise in the course of evolution by populations becoming isolated from each other, usually geographically, but sometimes by other means. Some of the other forms of biological isolation are well illustrated by these crickets. A species that is only adult in May and June, for example, cannot meet and mate with one that matures in July and August. Also, crickets are conditioned to respond only to the mating song of their own species; a female will not mate with a male who sings the "wrong" signature tune.

The so-called periodical cicada is one of the most famous of all North American insects because of its remarkable life-cycle of 13 or 17 years, almost all spent as a wingless larva underground. Here again recent research has shown that the situation is far less simple than formerly supposed.

There are six species of periodical cicada, three of them requiring 13 years to mature, the other three, 17 years. They are found in the eastern and central United States; in the southern part of the range all are 13-year cicadas, in the northern part all have the 17-year cycle, but there is a wide zone of overlap where both types occur. They do not appear all over the country at 17- or 13-year intervals, but various areas are occupied by broods that appear as adults in different years, the broods having become separated from each other in time, some time in the past, in some unknown way. Thus almost every year periodical cicadas appear somewhere in the United States. Each brood therefore represents a population that is isolated, for breeding purposes, from every other brood.

In addition to this extraordinary periodicity, each major brood of 13-year cicadas and each major brood of 17-year cicadas includes three species (six species in all) that remain distinct and do not interbreed.

Like crickets, cicadas communicate by singing. Their songs, uttered only by the males, seem to have the effect of bringing the males and females together in crowds. The greater the volume of noise the greater the attraction, the more cicadas singing the greater the noise, and so on in a chain reaction. It is fairly certain, too, that the insects recognize the voices of their own species and congregate accordingly. We have seen that a number of different factors combine to isolate and keep apart the cricket species, but voice recognition seems to be the only factor isolating the species of cicada within a particular brood, though the broods are isolated from each other very effectively. It is fairly easy to understand how the crickets have evolved in the way they have, but the case of the cicadas has no parallel anywhere else in the Animal Kingdom and is still by no means fully understood.

The small fireflies of the eastern United States, belonging to the genus *Photinus*, have been subjected to the same sort of intensive study in the field as the crickets and the periodical cicadas, and with equally interesting results. By observing the

These two maps show the distribution of the seven species of cricket belonging to the genus Gryllus *that live in North America. Above: South-eastern field-cricket (blue), northern spring and northern fall field-crickets (green), Jamaican field-cricket (light brown). Below: Southern wood-cricket (blue), northern wood-cricket (green), sand field-cricket (light brown).*

The map below shows the present distribution of the Colorado potato beetle.

The Colorado potato beetle is a pretty insect and only a little over a century ago was a harmless member of the fauna of the Rocky Mountains, feeding on a plant related to the potato. By intensive cultivation of potatoes man has provided an unnaturally favourable environment for it, and now, through no fault of its own, it is a pest. Colorado potato beetles are shown here at about three times actual size.

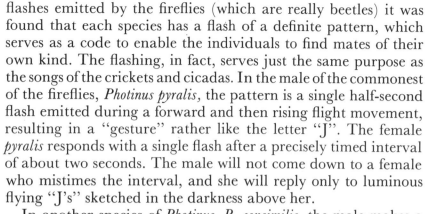

flashes emitted by the fireflies (which are really beetles) it was found that each species has a flash of a definite pattern, which serves as a code to enable the individuals to find mates of their own kind. The flashing, in fact, serves just the same purpose as the songs of the crickets and cicadas. In the male of the commonest of the fireflies, *Photinus pyralis*, the pattern is a single half-second flash emitted during a forward and then rising flight movement, resulting in a "gesture" rather like the letter "J". The female *pyralis* responds with a single flash after a precisely timed interval of about two seconds. The male will not come down to a female who mistimes the interval, and she will reply only to luminous flying "J's" sketched in the darkness above her.

In another species of *Photinus*, *P. consimilis*, the male makes a rapid succession of flashes and the female replies with two. By accident—if it is an accident—the female of another genus of larger fireflies, *Photurus*, has a very similar response signal, and *Photurus* females have quite often been found devouring a little male *Photinus consimilis*. It really looks as if these larger female fireflies have developed a predatory procedure almost exactly like that of the sirens of mythology, who devoured mariners, luring them to their doom by singing and seductive behaviour.

The early American settlers misnamed the cicadas "locusts," but as they pressed westward they soon found opportunities of using the term correctly. In the 1870's, the prairie States of North and South Dakota, Nebraska, and Kansas were visited by huge swarms of real locusts, and a farmer could be rendered destitute in a few hours if a swarm of them settled on his land. It was an age of piety and the locusts were generally regarded as being sent by Providence to chastise the people for their sins. The

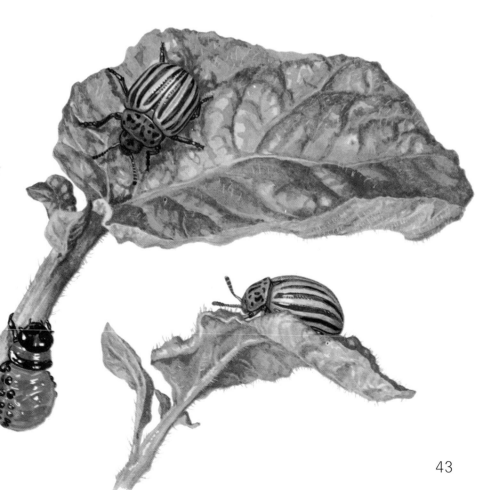

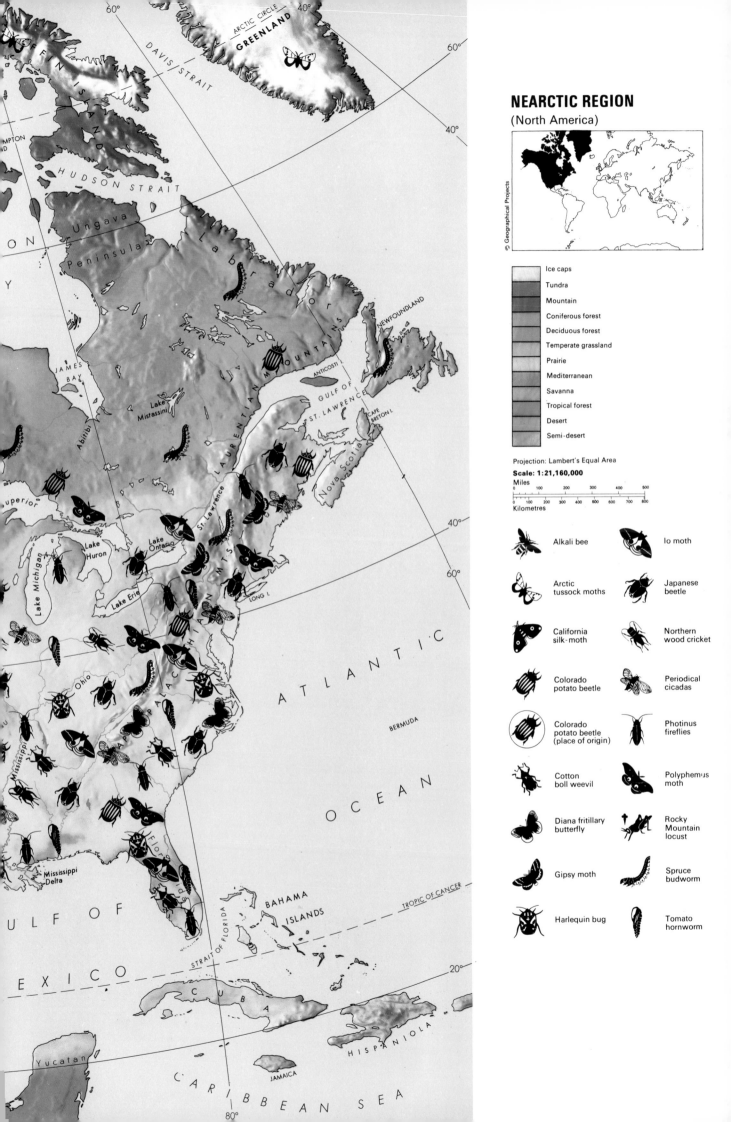

NEARCTIC REGION
(North America)

© Geographical Projects

	Ice caps
	Tundra
	Mountain
	Coniferous forest
	Deciduous forest
	Temperate grassland
	Prairie
	Mediterranean
	Savanna
	Tropical forest
	Desert
	Semi-desert

Projection: Lambert's Equal Area

Scale: 1:21,160,000

Miles
0 100 200 300 400 500

Kilometres
0 100 200 300 400 500 600 700 800

	Alkali bee		Io moth
	Arctic tussock moths		Japanese beetle
	California silk-moth		Northern wood cricket
	Colorado potato beetle		Periodical cicadas
	Colorado potato beetle (place of origin)		Photinus fireflies
	Cotton boll weevil		Polyphemus moth
	Diana fritillary butterfly		Rocky Mountain locust
	Gipsy moth		Spruce budworm
	Harlequin bug		Tomato hornworm

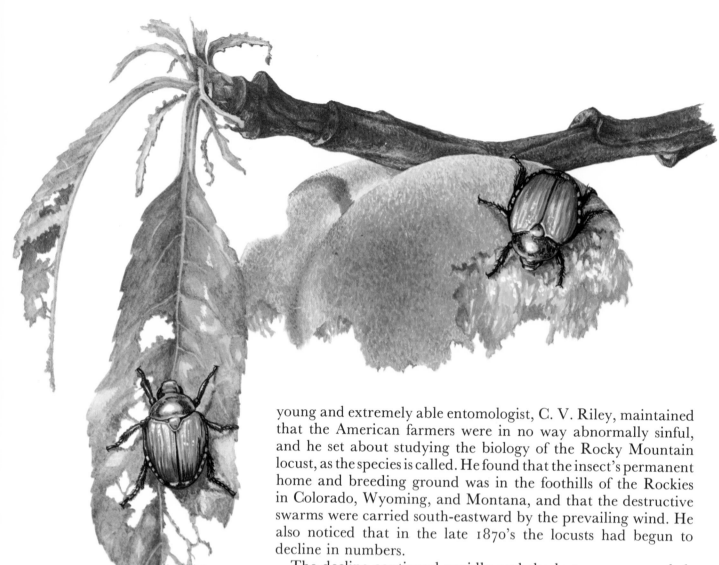

The Japanese beetle is one of the rather large number of insect species that have been accidentally introduced into the United States, and have flourished in their new habitat to the extent that they are now regarded as pests. It is a native of Japan and eastern China and made its way from Japan to America in soil around the roots of imported ornamental plants. It is allied to the cockchafer and has similar habits, feeding on roots as a larva and on the foliage, flowers, and fruit of a variety of plants when it becomes an adult beetle. It is shown here at about three times actual size.

young and extremely able entomologist, C. V. Riley, maintained that the American farmers were in no way abnormally sinful, and he set about studying the biology of the Rocky Mountain locust, as the species is called. He found that the insect's permanent home and breeding ground was in the foothills of the Rockies in Colorado, Wyoming, and Montana, and that the destructive swarms were carried south-eastward by the prevailing wind. He also noticed that in the late 1870's the locusts had begun to decline in numbers.

The decline continued rapidly and the last swarm recorded, a small one, was in 1892. A few specimens were collected during the next ten years, but since 1902 no one has seen a living Rocky Mountain locust, and the species is regarded as extinct. Evidently human settlement of their permanent breeding ground upset some ecological balance essential to their existence. Oddly enough, well-preserved specimens could still be collected long after 1902, for in a glacier in Montana, at an altitude of about 11,000 feet, huge numbers of the locusts were found preserved in layers in the ice, the remains, evidently, of swarms carried up through the high mountain pass by wind currents and numbed by the cold to the point of being unable to fly.

The Rocky Mountain locust has gone, but the Colorado potato beetle, also from the Rocky Mountains, is here to stay. It was first discovered in 1823 in the upper Missouri River region, feeding on the buffalo burr, a plant of the nightshade family, to which the potato also belongs. When the American West became settled, and potato culture was introduced there, the beetle transferred to it and multiplied prodigiously, changing its status from that of an entomological rarity to a major pest. It spread rapidly and was established along the Atlantic coast in 1874. By 1920 it had somehow got across to France, and now it is found all over Europe from Spain to western Russia. Outbreaks have occurred in Britain, but the beetle is not established there, and a constant watch is kept for it. It is unusual among insects in its wide tolerance of climate. It thrives in the desert country of Texas and survives the intensely cold winters of Canada and central Europe. It can probably live wherever man can grow potatoes.

America has inflicted the Colorado beetle on the world, but it has far more often been at the receiving end of intercontinental exchanges of harmful insects. In 1917, an exotic beetle appeared in a nursery garden near Philadelphia, and subsequent enquiry made it fairly certain that its eggs or larvae had arrived in soil around the roots of plants imported from Japan, where the beetle is common in both the north and south islands. It is also known from the vicinity of Canton in China. Japanese beetle is an obvious and suitable name for it. More precisely it is a member of the chafer family of beetles, allied to the cockchafer of the western Palaearctic region. Its feeding habits are normal for the family, the larva feeding underground on roots and the beetle itself on the leaves, flowers, and fruits of various plants.

Unfortunately, the beetle found living conditions in eastern North America very favourable, and, of course, it benefited from the absence of the parasitic insects that have evolved as its enemies in eastern Asia. Consequently, it multiplied enormously and is now a very serious pest in gardens and orchards, and on maize, or corn. A fruit tree may be completely stripped of leaves and flowers or fruit in 15 minutes by a swarm of Japanese beetles. The beetle attacks maize by devouring the "silk" of the developing cob. Its larvae are equally destructive underground.

The beautiful Diana fritillary is found in the southern and eastern United States from West Virginia south as far as Georgia and inland to the Mississippi valley. It is a woodland butterfly living in mountain and foothill country, and destruction of its habitat has greatly reduced its numbers in recent years. The remarkable difference in colour between the male and female is unique among fritillaries. It is believed that the blue female is a mimic of the pipe-vine swallowtail, a butterfly that is avoided by birds on account of the ill-tasting and poisonous properties derived from its food plant.

Specific parasites of the beetle have been sought out in Japan and introduced in attempts to control it. Some success has been achieved with a tiny parasitic wasp called *Tiphia*, and also with a bacterial disease, the spores of which are mixed with a neutral powder and introduced into the soil. Careful watch and control has slowed down the spread of Japanese beetles in America, but the watch should have been kept on the imported plants half a century ago.

The gipsy moth, a widely spread Palaearctic species, is one of the many harmful insects that have invaded North America from Europe. One curious story of its introduction relates that a French immigrant conceived the astonishing notion of crossing the gipsy with the common silk-moth and establishing a silk industry on this basis. Accordingly, in about 1870, he had eggs or cocoons sent across the Atlantic, bred stock from them (of course nothing profitable came of his venture), and inevitably some small larvae got carried away by the breeze. Whether or not it really got to America in this way, the moth was soon established in the region between the Great Lakes and the Atlantic Ocean and doing serious damage by defoliating a wide variety of orchard, parkland, and forest trees. One of the efforts to control it made use of the fact that the males are attracted to the females by a scent which she emits, and which a male can detect at a considerable distance. If the scent could be made available in quantity, males could be trapped and the females deprived of the means of fertilization. A total of 38,000 females was used to produce a sample sufficient for analysis, but it proved impossible to manufacture it synthetically. Parasitic flies imported from Europe have achieved some control of the gipsy moth and it has not spread widely. There seems good reason to hope that it will never menace the trees of the whole continent, which are falling all too fast before the saws and axes of human progress.

The butterflies of the Nearctic region reflect clearly its close zoogeographical affinity with the Palaearctic region. Although few species are common to the two regions, the general assemblage of North American butterflies consists of swallowtails, whites, yellows, vanessas, fritillaries, browns, coppers, blues, hairstreaks, and skippers, most of them having an aspect very much the same as their Palaearctic counterparts.

The Diana fritillary is a magnificent exception to this uniformity of appearance. The male and female are remarkably distinct, the male having the tawny and black coloration usual in fritillaries, while the female is bluish-black with light blue markings. The female has the distinction of being the only blue fritillary in the world.

Similarity between Palaearctic and Nearctic moths, which are far more diverse and numerous than butterflies, is also seen. The beautiful genus *Catocala*, for example, which includes the red and crimson underwings of Britain and Europe, is lavishly represented in North America, and there is also a fine variety of Saturniids, or emperors. Two large emperor species are widely spread and common. One of these is the cecropia, or robin, moth, whose larva feeds on a variety of trees, including willow,

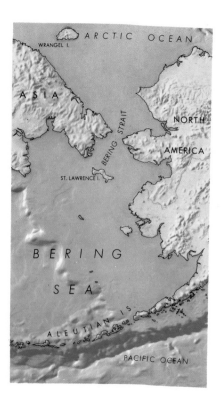

This map shows the shallow sea of the Bering Strait between Siberia and Alaska. In the remote past a land bridge probably joined the Palaearctic and Nearctic regions at this point, accounting for the similarity of some of the insects of the two regions.

By contrast with the Polyphemus moth the California, or mendocino, silk-moth has a limited distribution on the Pacific sea-board of North America. Both species are members of the emperor family, or Saturniidae. The California silk-moth is shown here at about twice actual size.

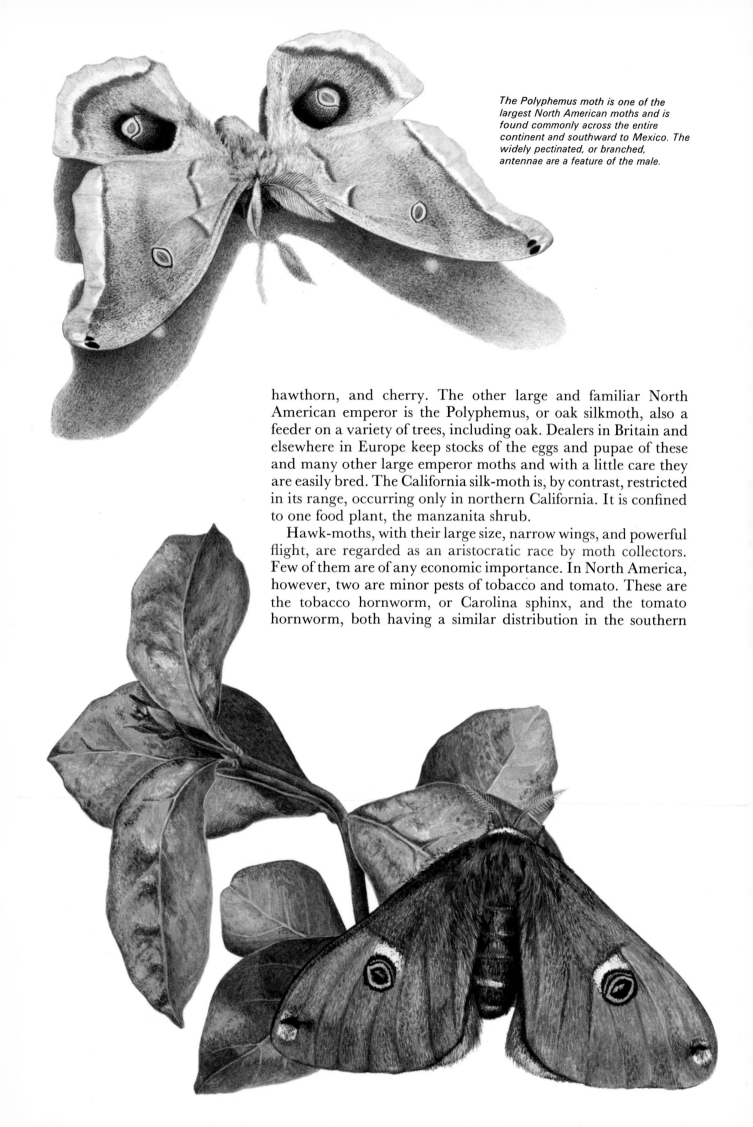

The Polyphemus moth is one of the largest North American moths and is found commonly across the entire continent and southward to Mexico. The widely pectinated, or branched, antennae are a feature of the male.

hawthorn, and cherry. The other large and familiar North American emperor is the Polyphemus, or oak silkmoth, also a feeder on a variety of trees, including oak. Dealers in Britain and elsewhere in Europe keep stocks of the eggs and pupae of these and many other large emperor moths and with a little care they are easily bred. The California silk-moth is, by contrast, restricted in its range, occurring only in northern California. It is confined to one food plant, the manzanita shrub.

Hawk-moths, with their large size, narrow wings, and powerful flight, are regarded as an aristocratic race by moth collectors. Few of them are of any economic importance. In North America, however, two are minor pests of tobacco and tomato. These are the tobacco hornworm, or Carolina sphinx, and the tomato hornworm, both having a similar distribution in the southern

The larvae of hawk-moths, or sphinx moths, are popularly called "hornworms" in America on account of the curved spike on their hinder ends. This species, the tomato hornworm, is a minor pest of tomato plants in the southern and eastern United States. In the pupa the moth's proboscis is contained in a hollow sheath having an appearance rather like the handle of a jug.

and eastern United States. The term "hornworm" refers to the curved horn on the tail of the big, green caterpillars, whose individual appetites are such that two or three of them will strip a tomato or tobacco plant of its leaves. The larvae bury themselves deeply in the ground to pupate. In the pupa stage, the long proboscis of the moth is contained in a tube that projects from the head, curves back and is attached at its end to a point a little forward of mid-way on the body, forming a feature looking like the handle of a jug.

If the hornworms are minor pests, the small brown moth that is the parent of the spruce budworm is certainly a major one. It is a native of the cool temperate part of North America and belongs to the same widespread group, the Tortricidea, as the codlin moth, the oriental peach moth, and other enemies of the gardener, farmer, and forester. The larvae of the spruce budworm feed on the needles of the terminal shoots of spruce, Douglas fir, larch, pine, and other coniferous trees. They may be present in enormous numbers and their feeding inhibits the growth of the trees and causes huge losses of timber. The larvae spin a web to hide in, and to hibernate in through the winter. The moths fly in July and August. Control is very difficult. Spraying or dusting insecticide powders from aeroplanes is widely practised, but it is not wholly effective and has to be done on such a large scale that it leads inevitably to environmental pollution, especially the poisoning of rivers. Research on biological control of the spruce budworm has been a preoccupation of entomologists for many years, and it is to be hoped that an effective parasite, bacillus, or virus will eventually be found.

Similarity to the Palaearctic fauna is modified by the northward invasion of the region by a number of insects of Neotropical origin. As might be expected these are most numerous in the southern Nearctic, but some have spread over most of its tem-

In the io moth the vividly ornamented hind-wings are covered by the fore-wings when the insect is at rest, making it quite inconspicuous. It is widespread in North America but most of its relatives live in the tropical regions of the New World.

perate area. One of these is the beautiful io moth, which has vivid eye spot markings on the hind-wings. Several close relatives, members of the same genus *Automeris*, are found in the southern states and many more live in Central and South America. The larva of the io feeds on a wide variety of trees and can be bred on linden, willow, elm, or poplar. This is another species of which dealers regularly stock larvae or pupae, often under the name "bull's-eye moth." It is delightful to breed such a beautiful insect in your home, but remember that the spines on the larva are poisonous and sting quite badly.

From the point of view of zoogeography the cotton boll weevil belongs to the transition zone between the Nearctic and Neotropical regions. It is a tiny brown beetle that spread northwards in the 1890's from Mexico, where it had been leading a blameless existence feeding on some wild relative of cotton. Its larvae live inside the bolls, or seed-cases, of the cotton plant and destroy both the seeds and the valuable fibres. They also pupate inside the bolls, so neither larva nor pupa can effectively be reached by insecticides. The adult weevils can be killed with a poisonous dust, best applied by low-flying aeroplanes, and cleaning up and burning all rubbish in the cotton fields destroys many overwintering weevils, but these measures come nowhere near eradicating it. Nevertheless, in spite of the enormously costly damage it does, it has probably had a beneficial effect on the economy of the Southern States.

Before its arrival, Southern agriculture was too intensively concentrated on two crops, cotton and tobacco, and the boll weevil persuaded the cotton farmers to diversify their agriculture, setting a good example to the rest. One Southern city has even gone to the length of erecting a statue to the weevil in recognition of its rather drastic good services.

The harlequin bug, a North American member of the family Pentatomidae, colloquially known as shieldbugs or stinkbugs, has spread northwards from Texas, where it was first discovered. Members of this insect family generally have the shape of a heraldic shield and also have a disgusting odour, which serves to protect them against predation. Many have vivid warning coloration, including the harlequin bug, which is boldly marked with red or orange and black. Unfortunately, it is a serious pest of cabbage and allied plants. The eggs are very curious, looking like tiny white barrels with black rings, and the young resemble the adults in miniature, except that they lack wings and have the black-and-orange markings differently disposed. Shieldbugs are often confused with beetles, but their mode of development is totally different. All beetles go through larva and pupa stages before reaching the adult form; the true bugs, or Hemiptera, never do so. In the south, the harlequin bug is active the year round. In the northern part of its range it hides away in winter, coming out to feed on warm days.

From insect pests we turn now to an example of how insects can help the farmer. Bees are economically far more important as pollinators of the plants of agriculture than as producers of honey. Only one kind of bee produces honey on a large scale, but pollination is effected by a great variety of wild bees as well as by the domestic honeybee. Most plants are well served by the honeybee and hives are often placed in orchards at blossom time to this end, but there are some important crops whose flowers are not effectively pollinated by honeybees. One of these is alfalfa, or lucerne. When grown in America for its seed yield, it was found that alfalfa was only successful in rather wild, sparsely populated country. The reason for this was that its only effective pollinators are small solitary bees whose numbers, like those of almost all wild creatures, dwindle with the coming of agriculture and human habitation.

One of the best of these alfalfa bees is a small species known as the alkali bee, a native of the more arid areas of western North America. It nests in salty or alkaline soil, making its burrows just below the surface in pockets where the humidity is high. It is a gregarious breeder, nesting in crowds, with the burrows close together. Ploughing, drainage, and other accompaniments of civilization tend to destory its breeding grounds, and so it is seldom naturally available just where the farmers want it.

Professor W. P. Stephen of the University of Oregon conceived the ingenious idea of constructing artificial "bee-beds" for the alkali bee, simulating as closely as possible the conditions under which it breeds naturally. After much research, a design was perfected. The bed was about 30 feet square and 3 feet deep, with a polythene base. A 4-inch layer of gravel was spread over the base and the bed filled with soil of suitable consistency. Salt was mixed in at the surface and water poured down spouts to the gravel, giving the proper below-surface humidity. In the spring, soil blocks from natural breeding grounds, containing large numbers of overwintering larvae, were transported to the artificial bed. These produced bees, which emerged and continued burrowing and nesting in the bed until the whole of it was occupied, with a final density of 1,000 to 1,500 nesting females per square yard.

The combined effect of these artificial bee-beds and of conservation of natural sites in Oregon has resulted in yields of alfalfa seed up to 2,000 pounds per acre. The average previous yield in the United States was 175 to 200 pounds per acre. Economic entomology is all too often directed towards destruction of wildlife, and it is pleasant to encounter an example of research to promote a profitable alliance between farmers and an insect.

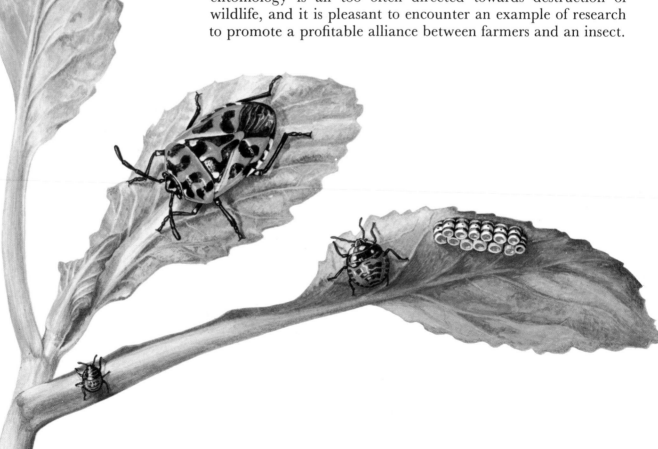

4
The
Oriental
Region

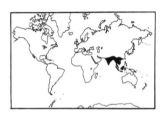

Tropical Asia, including the islands of Ceylon and the East Indies archipelago east to Borneo and Bali, the Philippines, and some of the adjacent, smaller islands.

This is the only one of the zoogeographical regions that lies almost entirely within the tropics. It comprises Asia south of the Palaearctic region, the large islands standing on the Sunda Shelf (Borneo, Sumatra, Java), and the Philippines. Celebes and the Lesser Sunda Islands, as far east as Timor, form a zone of transition to the Australian region, and there is a transition to the Palaearctic region westward in Iran. The Himalayas and their eastern and western extensions form an east to west barrier between the Palaearctic and the Oriental regions.

The giant honeybee is a typical Oriental insect, occurring over all the most easterly part of the region and not at all outside it. It is one of the few tropical relatives of the domesticated honeybee, but is larger and is distinguished by an orange patch at the base of the abdomen. The nest consists of a single comb hanging vertically and usually high above the ground. Nests are often attached to the underside of a thick branch of one of the towering trees that make up the rain forest, a hundred feet or more overhead. As many as 65 combs have been counted in a single tree; as there may be as many as 70,000 cells in a single comb, a tree can support a large population of the bees. The combs are sometimes suspended from the roofs of high caves or in places where cliffs overhang. Buildings are frequently used, especially bridges and water towers that have a central column and a large elevated reservoir that projects all round. In these situations, too, there may be numerous combs hanging quite close together, but each one of them is a separate colony.

The cells are disposed horizontally and point outwards on each side of the comb. They are all of the same size, those in which the drones and queens develop being no larger than the ones in which larvae of workers grow up. The queens and drones

Leaf- and stick-insects are large and usually slow moving, and so must rely mainly on concealment for protection from their enemies. Leaf-insects, especially, afford a remarkable example of natural camouflage. Both body and legs of the leaf-insect are flattened to resemble leaves and their surfaces are coloured and patterned to the same end. The elongated bodies of stick-insects look like twigs without further adaptation, but the resemblance is enhanced by appropriate colours and postures. The enormous giant stick-insect (top) is one of the largest insects known. The laboratory stick-insect (centre left) is often kept in captivity.

are, indeed, not much bigger than the workers; in the domesticated honeybee they are noticeably larger. Another distinction from the honeybee lies in the fact that the combs are not permanent colonies. If conditions become unfavourable, due to a temporary shortage of trees in flower nearby or a spell of bad weather, all the bees will abandon the comb and make a new one elsewhere. This is the chief reason why the giant honeybee has so far proved impossible to domesticate.

This bee is sometimes dangerous when the workers attack in large numbers, and human deaths are reported from time to time from this hazard. The bees normally take no notice of people walking below the nest, but a bird of prey, the honey buzzard, has the habit of feeding on the larvae, honey, and wax in the combs. The buzzard simply tears the nest to pieces, being in some way protected against the stings, but the bees are driven to a frenzy and will attack anything moving in the vicinity. If you ever see a bees' nest being attacked by a large bird in the eastern tropics, do not on any account approach to get a better view.

In spite of the formidable nature of giant honeybees the nests are regularly raided for honey by the jungle-dwelling people of Borneo. Usually a bamboo ladder is built up to the nest at night, and the climber is equipped with a smoky torch to keep off the bees. Nevertheless, it is a feat that needs the body of an athlete and the courage of a warrior.

The dwarf honeybee also is an Oriental insect, smaller than the domestic species, but with nesting habits rather like those of the giant honeybee. It, too, builds a single comb hanging from a branch, but here there are differences in the cells, which are of four sizes. Near the top of the comb are cells for storing honey and below them a zone of smaller cells in which worker larvae are reared. Below this are larger cells for drone larvae and hanging from the bottom of the comb are queen cells, the largest of all. The honey, worker, and drone cells are all hexagonal in shape, but the big queen cells are irregularly cylindrical.

The atlas moth is common in most parts of the region and in the islands to the east, almost as far as New Guinea. It is a magnificent insect, one of the largest of all moths, sometimes attaining a span of ten inches across the wings. It belongs to the family Saturniidae, which also includes the European emperor and the North American Polyphemus moths. Atlas moths often come into houses at night, attracted by the lights, and may cause alarm or joy according to the temperament of the observer. The huge, pale-green caterpillars often appear on garden shrubs and may strip off all the leaves by the time they are ready to pupate. They feed on a wide variety of shrubs and trees, and can be reared in temperate countries on a diet of privet, willow, or rhododendron leaves, but a constant temperature of 70° to 80°F. is necessary.

Raja Brooke's birdwing is as outstanding among the Oriental butterflies as the atlas is among the moths, and its distribution serves to illustrate an interesting feature of Oriental zoogeography. The Malay Peninsula is joined to continental

The magnificent atlas moth is shown here at actual size. It is common over most of the Oriental region and often flies into lighted houses. The caterpillars feed on a great variety of trees and shrubs, and a dozen of them may strip the leaves of a garden bush in the course of their rapid growth.

Asia at the south-west corner of Thailand, and the part of it comprising West Malaysia lies between the two great islands of Sumatra and Borneo. If the animal life (not only the insects) of the peninsula is compared with that of the adjoining continent on the one hand and with the Greater Sunda Islands—Sumatra, Borneo, and Java—on the other, the fauna of the peninsula is found to have far more in common with the islands than with the mainland.

At first sight this seems hard to explain; the peninsula is connected with the continent and cut off from the islands by the sea. The key to the puzzle is provided by submarine soundings taken all over the area. These reveal that a line drawn closely around Sumatra, Java, and Borneo, taking in the Philippine island of Palawan and extended to the continent on either side of the Malay Peninsula, contains an area of quite shallow sea. Outside this line the depth increases rapidly. The peninsula and the islands are in fact standing on a great shelf, jutting out from the corner of Southeast Asia and requiring only a slight elevation of the land or recession of the sea to convert it into an enormous broadly connected peninsula of continuous land. Evidently it existed in this form for some millions of years of fairly recent geological time, but erosion slowly lowered its mountains and deepened its valleys until large areas of it approached sea level. Its fragmentation was finally brought about by the conditions

prevailing in the last Ice Age. During the periods of glaciation, when the cool temperate parts of the earth were covered with thick sheets of ice, so much water was withdrawn from the oceans that the world sea level fell 200 to 300 feet below that of today. This relative heightening of the land gave new life to rivers and hastened erosion, so that when the seas finally rose again, about 10,000 years ago, the great Sundaland Peninsula was largely flooded and only its higher parts remained as dry land.

One of the most splendid of all butterflies, Raja Brooke's birdwing, inhabits a rather restricted area within the Oriental region. Males (as shown here) may often be seen on the ground drinking the water of seepages and saline springs, but the female flies high among the trees.

This relief map shows the shallow continental shelf, called the Sunda Shelf, on which Sumatra, Java, Borneo, Palawan, and the Malay Peninsula stand. The area once formed a huge peninsula above sea level, with an assemblage of animals largely of its own. This explains why some insects of the small peninsula of West Malaysia are also found on the Sunda Islands but not elsewhere in the Oriental region.

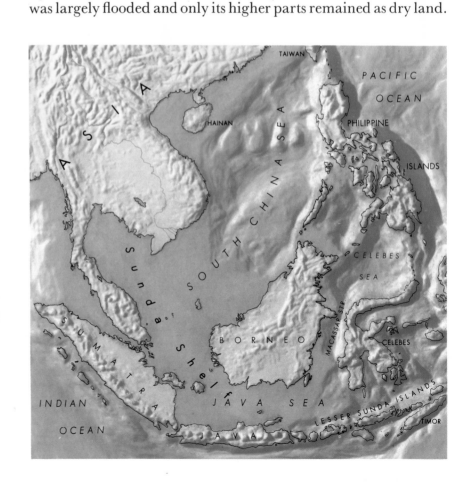

During its long existence, this great equatorial land mass, with a climate differing noticeably from that of the main continent to the north, developed an assemblage of animals largely of its own, and many of them survive today on the islands and the relatively small peninsula of West Malaysia, which are all that remain of Sundaland. These are now regarded as forming a zoological subregion within the Oriental region.

This is an over-simplified account of its history, and among the many complications that occurred was the cutting off of Java by the sea some time before the severance of Sumatra and Borneo. It is this that accounts for the distribution of Raja Brooke's birdwing on the Malay Peninsula and all the Sunda Islands except Java. It was discovered in Sarawak in 1854 by the English naturalist A. R. Wallace and named by him after Sir James Brooke, first of the "white rajas," who ruled Sarawak until 1941.

In the tropical forests examples of adaptive form and coloration aimed at concealment, commonly called camouflage, are numerous and often very striking and perfect. The stick- and leaf-insects, for example, are abundant and varied in the Oriental forests. They are rather large, sluggish insects whose only hope of survival lies in concealment, and some of them afford extraordinary examples of cryptic form and coloration.

The attenuated body and long legs of the stick-insects can simulate twigs, grass-stems and the like without much special modification, but perfection is often achieved by the peculiar attitudes that the insects assume when at rest. Their bodies are usually green or brown, and in some kinds the tone can be darkened or lightened by the spreading or clumping of pigment granules in the skin. This can be observed if laboratory stick-insects (the species most often kept in captivity) are confined with dark and light backgrounds. Some stick-insects are among the largest of all insects. These include one with the name

The Indian leaf butterfly affords a beautiful example of natural camouflage. When it is at rest its wings exactly simulate a dead leaf, the mid-rib being represented by a dark line running continuously across fore- and hind-wings. The stalk is formed by the "tails" on the hind-wings.

ORIENTAL REGION
(South Asia)

© Geographical Projects

Mountain
Coniferous forest
Deciduous forest
Temperate grassland
Prairie
Mediterranean
Savanna
Tropical forest
Desert
Semi-desert
Fertile lands

Projection: Lambert's Azimuthal Equal Area

Scale: 1:21,600,000

Miles
100 200 300 400 500 600
Kilometres
100 200 300 400 500 600 700 800 900 1000 1100

Atlas moth

Branded imperial butterfly

Coconut beetle
(Rhinoceros beetle)

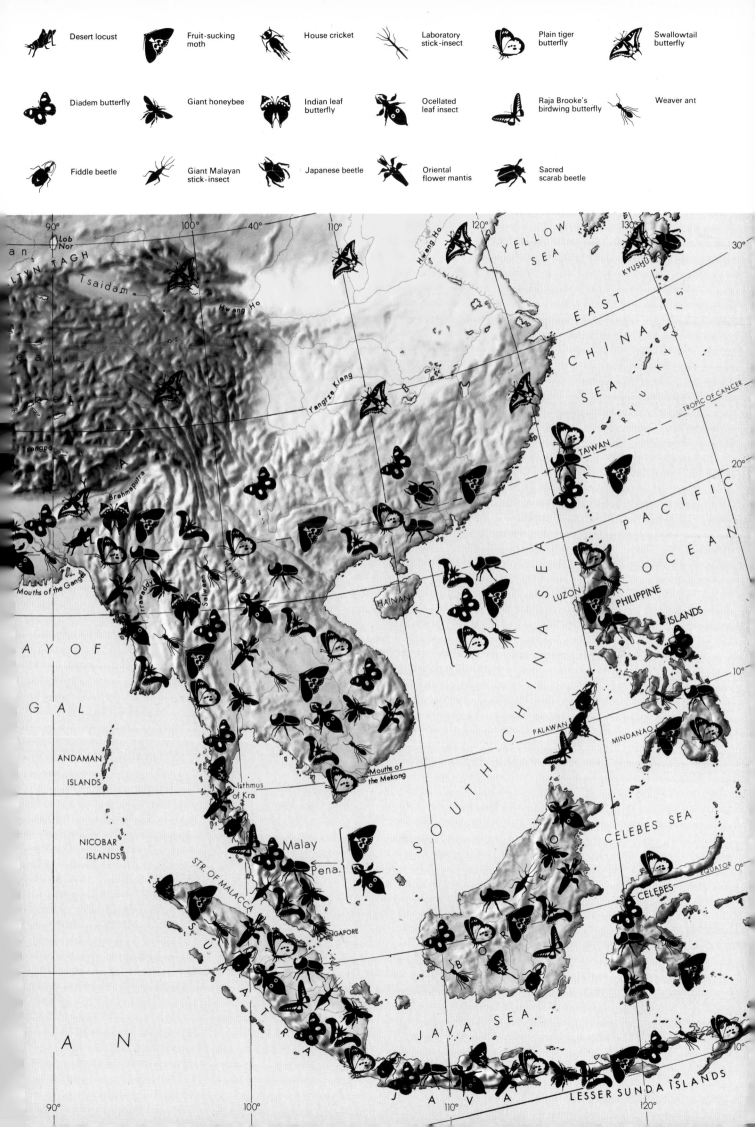

Desert locust
Fruit-sucking moth
House cricket
Laboratory stick-insect
Plain tiger butterfly
Swallowtail butterfly

Diadem butterfly
Giant honeybee
Indian leaf butterfly
Ocellated leaf insect
Raja Brooke's birdwing butterfly
Weaver ant

Fiddle beetle
Giant Malayan stick-insect
Japanese beetle
Oriental flower mantis
Sacred scarab beetle

In the stages just before it comes to maturity the remarkable Oriental flower mantis is coloured pink and closely resembles a large pink flower. This resemblance serves two purposes; birds that would like to make a meal of the mantis are deceived, and flower-loving insects, such as flies, are attracted and are seized and eaten when they approach too near. In the creamy-white adult the resemblance to a flower is largely lost.

Palophus titan whose body is a foot long, and also massive species such as the giant Malayan stick-insect shown on page 55.

The leaf-insects afford some of the most extreme examples of concealment by simulation of a natural object. They are green and have the sides of the body and some of the leg-joints flattened, and the fore-wings have a net-like texture exactly like that formed by the veins of a leaf. In addition, there are often spots and blemishes that look just like the marks on leaves caused by galls or fungus.

The Indian leaf butterfly is found in the western part of the Oriental region, but has close relatives to the east, on the Sunda Islands. When the butterfly is at rest the colour and texture of the underside of the wings closely resemble a dead leaf, and the outline of the two wings together simulates the outline of a leaf, with the short "tail" on the hind-wings representing the leaf-stalk. Nor is this all; a dark line, crossing both wings from fore-wing tip to hind-wing tail, simulates the mid-rib of the leaf, and the continuity of this line is determined by the relative positions of the two wings in the butterfly's natural resting pose. This coincident pattern on the two wings is a refinement of camouflage only occasionally seen in nature.

The Oriental flower-mantis is a remarkable-looking insect when fully grown. It is creamy-white and has the large joints of the two hinder pairs of legs broad and flattened. The forelegs are modified for seizing prey as in all mantises. The body is long and straight with fully developed wings. The younger stages of this mantis, before the skin is cast for the last time, are much more extraordinary. Here the wings are short and of no use for flying, the hinder part of the body is carried bent forward over the back and the whole insect is pale pink in colour. The effect is almost perfect simulation of a flower, the four leg expansions representing the petals and the body a rather complicated centre

The Oriental flower-mantis has been observed sitting on a flower of the Singapore rhododendron, but it does not seem necessary for it to do this in order to exploit its adaptation. If it

When the little branded imperial butterfly is at rest birds are deceived by the form and markings of the hind-wings and make their predatory grab there, under the impression that they are seizing the butterfly's head.

just sat among the foliage it would certainly look much more like a flower than any sort of insect. Its elaborate camouflage serves a double purpose. It is concealed from recognition by large insectivorous birds and also such insects as butterflies on which it feeds. In fact its flower-like appearance probably serves actually to attract its prey. Indeed, flies (but not butterflies) have been observed to approach and settle on it and to be seized and devoured as a consequence.

The little branded imperial butterfly belongs to the same family as the blues and hairstreaks, the Lycaenidae. It is a true inhabitant of the ancient Sundaland, for it now lives only in the jungles of the Malay Peninsula and on the islands of the Shelf, and nowhere else. It illustrates a mode of self-protection found here and there in nature which, by a little stretching of the usual meaning of the word "camouflage," can be called "back-to-front camouflage." The very long white "tails" on the hind-wings are its most noticeable feature, and in side view it is obvious that the pattern becomes more conspicuous towards the hind border of the hind-wings, culminating in bold black spots and finally in the long feathery tails. It is easy to imagine the attention of a bird or lizard, when stalking a resting branded imperial butterfly, being directed towards this area of the wings and away from the insect's head and body. It may even take the tails for the butterfly's antennae and be deluded into supposing that the insect is facing in this direction. Accordingly it makes its predatory grab at the base of the tails, seizing the wings and missing its victim's body altogether. After a brief struggle the fragile wings tear away and the butterfly, left with a wing area quite adequate for flight, makes its escape. To be sure the device will only work once, but in a butterfly's short lifetime one escape from death is well worth having.

Among the burnet moths, which were discussed in Chapter 2,

The male and female of the diadem butterfly (top left and top right) are totally different in appearance, but the female bears a close resemblance to the plain tiger butterfly (bottom), in which the sexes are similar, and which belongs to another family of butterflies, the Danaidae. All the species of this family are poisonous to birds, which learn to recognize them and avoid eating them. The perfectly edible female diadem gains protection from the resemblance.

we encountered a case of protection by possession of foul tasting and poisonous body fluids, accompanied by warning coloration. As one might expect, this is frequent among tropical insects, including some of the butterflies. In most of these the larva feeds on some poisonous plant and the chemical substance concerned persists in the insect's body through the pupa stage to the adult. As a rule entire families or genera have this mode of protection, not random species in the whole range of butterflies. One such family is the Danaidae, the "tigers" and "crows" of Asia, which also includes the well known American monarch. All the Danaids are poisonous and all the species have a distinctive appearance.

Here and there among butterflies of other families such as the Nymphalidae (which are never protected by inedible properties), one encounters species that resemble some Danaid species or other so closely as to rule out any possibility of pure coincidence. More remarkable still, it is often only the female of the palatable species that resembles the inedible one. A case of this kind is illustrated on page 63. A specimen of the plain tiger, a Danaid butterfly in which the sexes are alike, is shown with a male and female of the diadem butterfly (a member of the Nymphalidae). The male diadem has an appearance quite normal for the genus (*Hypolimnas*) to which it belongs, while the female is utterly unlike her mate and so closely resembles the plain tiger that the two require quite careful examination to separate them.

Numerous cases of resemblance of this kind are known among tropical butterflies, and other animals as well, and they illustrate the phenomenon of protective mimicry. Birds learn to avoid the

The weaver ant makes its nest among trees and bushes, using a method of construction unique among insects. Leaves are joined together with silk, but the ants cannot produce the silk themselves. Only their larvae can do this. They are held in the jaws of the worker ants, and a thread of silk exudes from each larva as it is passed to and fro between the leaves.

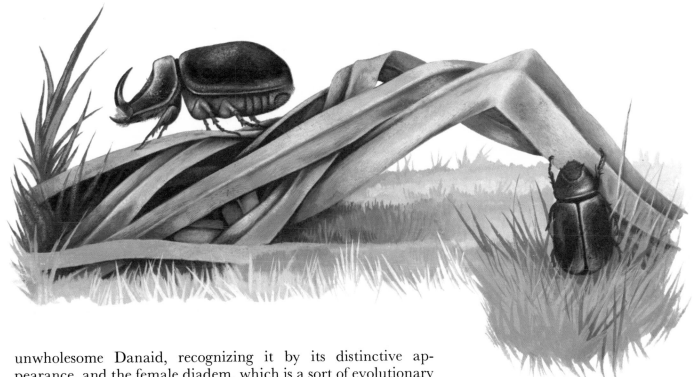

unwholesome Danaid, recognizing it by its distinctive appearance, and the female diadem, which is a sort of evolutionary counterfeit, gains protection as well. In such an association the genuinely inedible form is called the model and the deceiver the mimic, and experiments in aviaries have shown that birds are indeed deceived. If the mimics were too numerous birds would soon learn that not all butterflies with the appearance of the model are inedible, and it is a fact that the mimetic species are generally rarer than the models in territories in which both of them fly. For the same reason it is to the advantage of the mimic if the resemblance is limited to the female, since she needs a longer life than the male to complete her part in propagating the species. This is not always the case; sometimes both sexes of a butterfly are mimetic. In other cases, several distinct forms of the female of a mimetic species exist, each resembling a different inedible species.

The coconut palm is of great economic importance in tropical countries, and a number of insects feed on and damage the tree. The rhinoceros beetle is one of the most widespread of these pests.

The typical form of the weaver ant is an Oriental insect, though distinct subspecies are found in the Philippines and eastward in the Australian region. They are rusty-red, long-legged, fairly large ants that make their nests in trees or bushes by joining living leaves together with silk. They attack anyone who brushes against the branch bearing the nest, biting with their jaws and ejecting an acrid fluid over the wound. It is the workers that are red, the queens being bright green (a most unusual colour among ants) and the males black.

The making of the nest involves an extraordinary procedure. The ants themselves have no means of producing silk, but the larvae have silk glands, evolved originally, no doubt, to enable them to make cocoons when they pupate. But no weaver ant larva ever makes a cocoon. Instead, its silk is used for the good of the community. When a leaf is to be added to the nest, or a breach repaired, a number of workers seize the edges to be joined and hold them in the required position while other workers enter the nest and bring out living larvae. These, squeezed gently in their grown-up sisters' jaws (workers are females), are passed to and fro between the edges in such a way that a web of silk is spun across the space, the larvae being used like the shuttle of a loom or a tube of glue.

Coconuts are an important crop around the coasts of the Oriental region, and the products of the coconut palm are of great importance in the domestic economy of the Asian people, who use the fronds for thatching, the oil for cooking, the fibre for matting and string, and the sugary sap for making a wholesome, mildly alcoholic beverage called toddy. The dried flesh of the nut, called copra, is of economic importance as a source of vegetable oil.

Like all cultivated plants the coconut has insect pests specific to it. One of these is a large black beetle called the rhinoceros beetle, so named because the male has a curved erect horn on its head. The adult insect is about two inches long and does serious harm by boring into the crown of the palms, damaging the terminal bud and opening the way for other pests to enter. Its larva, a large white grub, does not harm the palm trees, but feeds in decaying vegetable matter such as rotten logs or the crowns of dead palms. It is rather unusual for insect pests to be harmful in the adult stage and relatively harmless as a larva. Careful clearing up and burning of all plant debris on coconut plantations is the best means of controlling the rhinoceros beetle.

Moths and butterflies feed when adult (if they feed at all) by sucking liquid through a long tubular proboscis, which curls up under the head when not in use, when it looks like the hairspring of a watch. The nectar of flowers is their most usual food, though many of them also relish the sweet excretions—or "honeydew"—of aphids and the juices of crushed or broken fruits. One group of moths, well represented in the Oriental region, has the proboscis stiff and sharp and uses it to pierce the rind of undamaged fruit and suck out the juice. One of these, the common fruit-sucking moth, is a beautiful insect with an extremely wide range from the northern part of the Australian region through the Oriental region to tropical Africa. It feeds on

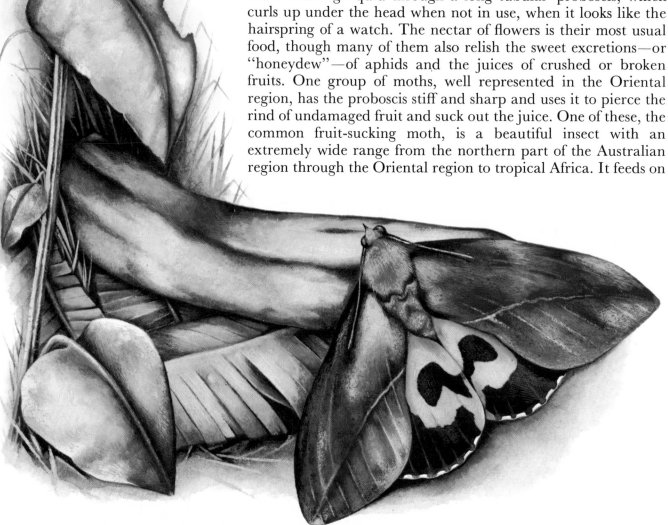

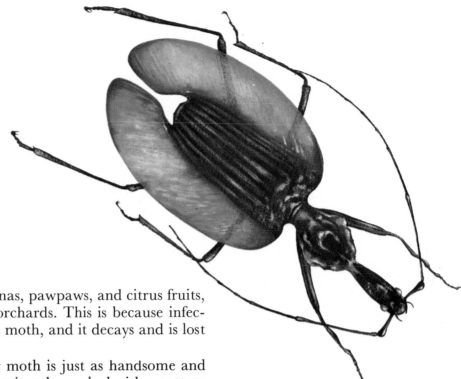

all kinds of fruits including bananas, pawpaws, and citrus fruits, and does considerable harm in orchards. This is because infection enters any fruit pierced by a moth, and it decays and is lost to the market.

The larva of the fruit-sucking moth is just as handsome and striking as the adult insect. It is intricately marked with a pattern of red and brown in different shades and has, on each side of two of the forward segments of the body, a sharply outlined and black-centred eye-like spot. If it is molested it curls the head under the body so that the whole front half of the caterpillar forms a closed ring with the eye-like spots on its upper part. At the same time the tail end is raised. The creature no longer looks like an insect but presents an image suggesting the front part of a snake with swollen head and glaring eyes. In the tropics tree-snakes are deadly enemies of birds and lizards, and an appearance calling to mind that of a snake, even if the resemblance is not exact, could well be enough to alarm and repel one of these equally deadly enemies of caterpillars. Other cases are known of snake mimicry by larvae of butterflies and moths, some of them even showing precise resemblance to particular kinds of snakes, and there is little doubt that it provides some measure of protection.

Our last example of an Oriental insect is yet another inhabitant of the ancient Sundaland and is one of the oddest-looking beetles known. The large, flat, translucent expansions on each side of the body of the fiddle beetle are projections of the wing-cases, or elytra. They have never been explained in terms of adaptation, and we must accept this extraordinary insect as a curiosity of the evolutionary process that we do not yet understand. Fiddle beetles are carnivorous and use their elongated heads to probe in crevices for small insects. Their larvae have been found living in tunnels in the large bracket fungi that grow commonly in the humid forests.

When fiddle beetles were first discovered, high prices were paid for specimens. They are not really rare, but if clearing of their rain-forest habitat goes on at the present rate these insects and many others will disappear for ever. Specimens of them, sad relics of former luxuriance, will then regain their former value.

5 The Ethiopian Region

Africa south of the Sahara Desert (excluding the island of Madagascar) and the south-western tip of Arabia. The Sahara Desert forms a transitional zone to the Palaearctic region.

At the present time this region is biologically isolated by desert to the north and by the oceans in other directions. The northern barrier has, however, not been of nearly such long duration as the ocean barriers that cut off the Ethiopian region from the Neotropical and the Australian regions. Of the three wholly or largely southern habitable continents the Ethiopian has, in regard to its insects, most in common with the great northern land masses. The affinities are strongest with the Oriental region, many genera and even a number of species being common to the two regions.

If an insect had to be selected as symbolic of Africa, a suitable if rather macabre choice would be the tsetse fly. The term applies not to a single species but to the members of a genus of flies called *Glossina*, restricted to the Ethiopian region and spread all over the tropical parts of it where the rainfall exceeds 20 inches a year. In the past tsetse flies have had a profound retarding influence on the development of human culture in tropical Africa. Until the advent of machines their presence restricted travelling and transport to the speed of walking and to loads carried on men's heads, and agriculture to laborious tillage with the hoe.

All of them feed on the blood of vertebrate animals, mainly large mammals including man, and unlike mosquitoes and horse flies, the male as well as the female tsetse is a bloodsucker. They carry a variety of protozoan parasites called trypanosomes that alternate in their life history between the flies and their victims and are conveyed into and out of their blood stream by the flies' habit of injecting and sucking back saliva when they bite. Two species of trypanosome cause the terrible human disease sleeping sickness and three other species are responsible for the

The Goliath beetle, shown here at life size, is possibly the bulkiest and heaviest insect in the world, though the tropical American Hercules beetle is very nearly as big. It is found in western tropical Africa and its larvae live in rotting wood. The Goliath beetle is a giant relative of the pretty metallic green cetonia, or rose-chafer, and of the North American green June beetle.

deadly nagana which is rapidly fatal to horses and cattle. It is impossible to protect grazing animals from infection; they simply cannot live in areas inhabited by infected tsetse flies. The native African animals harbour the disease-causing trypanosomes but are immune to their effects, and they therefore constitute a reservoir of nagana and sleeping sickness. The lamentable expedient of completely exterminating game animals has been resorted to as a means of controlling the diseases, but is seldom more than partly or temporarily effective.

The breeding habits of tsetse flies are most unusual. A single egg hatches into a larva while still in the uterus of the female and is nourished by a secretion derived from her frequent blood meals. When it is fully grown the fly gives birth to the larva, which immediately burrows into the ground and pupates and shortly afterwards hatches into a fly. A female tsetse fly produces no more than a dozen progeny in her life (far less than a female rabbit) and yet these insects are so abundant as to be a scourge over an area of Africa half as great again as that of the United States.

An account has been given in Chapter 2 of the desert locust, the most important and destructive of the "plague" locusts. This species invades the Ethiopian region southward to Uganda and Kenya in the east and Nigeria in the west. South of this line two other species are, or rather were, a serious threat to human subsistence. The African migratory locust has invaded almost the whole of the continent south of the Sahara at one time or another. The red locust is a more southern insect, having its northern limit in Zaire to the west and extending its swarms through Kenya into Somalia in the east.

The migratory locust was the subject of the earliest research on phase variation, which was mentioned briefly when we discussed the desert locust. At the beginning of the century it was thought that there were two species involved in the occurrence of migratory locusts (using the term in its specific sense, since all plague locusts migrate), differing in structure and coloration as

The inset map shows tsetse fly distribution (brown) and the area with more than 20 inches of rainfall a year (within red lines).

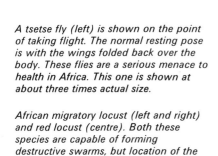

A tsetse fly (left) is shown on the point of taking flight. The normal resting pose is with the wings folded back over the body. These flies are a serious menace to health in Africa. This one is shown at about three times actual size.

African migratory locust (left and right) and red locust (centre). Both these species are capable of forming destructive swarms, but location of the areas where the swarms originate has made it possible to control them.

well as in habits. Then, in 1912, B. P. Uvarov, a Russian entomologist, bred locusts of one "species" from eggs of the other, and realized that only one species was involved which was capable of existing in two distinct forms, or phases. Uvarov had to leave Russia at the time of the Bolshevik Revolution and settled in England, where he became the world's leading figure in locust research. His work and that of his colleagues in London has saved millions of people from misery and death through famine caused by swarming locusts.

The growth of a locust into one or the other phase has nothing to do with its parentage, but depends simply upon whether it grows up in crowded conditions or develops with little or no contact with others of its species. In the migratory locust the most conspicuous difference between the two is in the coloration of the young insects, or hoppers. Those of the solitary phase are uniform green or brown, the colour matching the background in which they grow up. The gregarious hoppers have a bold pattern of black and yellow or orange markings. The winged adults of the two phases differ less strikingly in colour but display structural differences. The principal one concerns the relative length of the fore-wing and the thigh, or femur, of the hind leg. In the solitary phase the wing is always less than twice as long as the femur; whereas in locusts developing from gregarious phase, brightly coloured hoppers the wing is more than twice as long. Gregarious phase adults have larger eyes, a differently shaped thorax and the sexes are equal in size, the male being much smaller in the solitary phase. There was indeed every excuse for thinking they were two distinct species. In

71

ETHIOPIAN REGION
(North Africa)

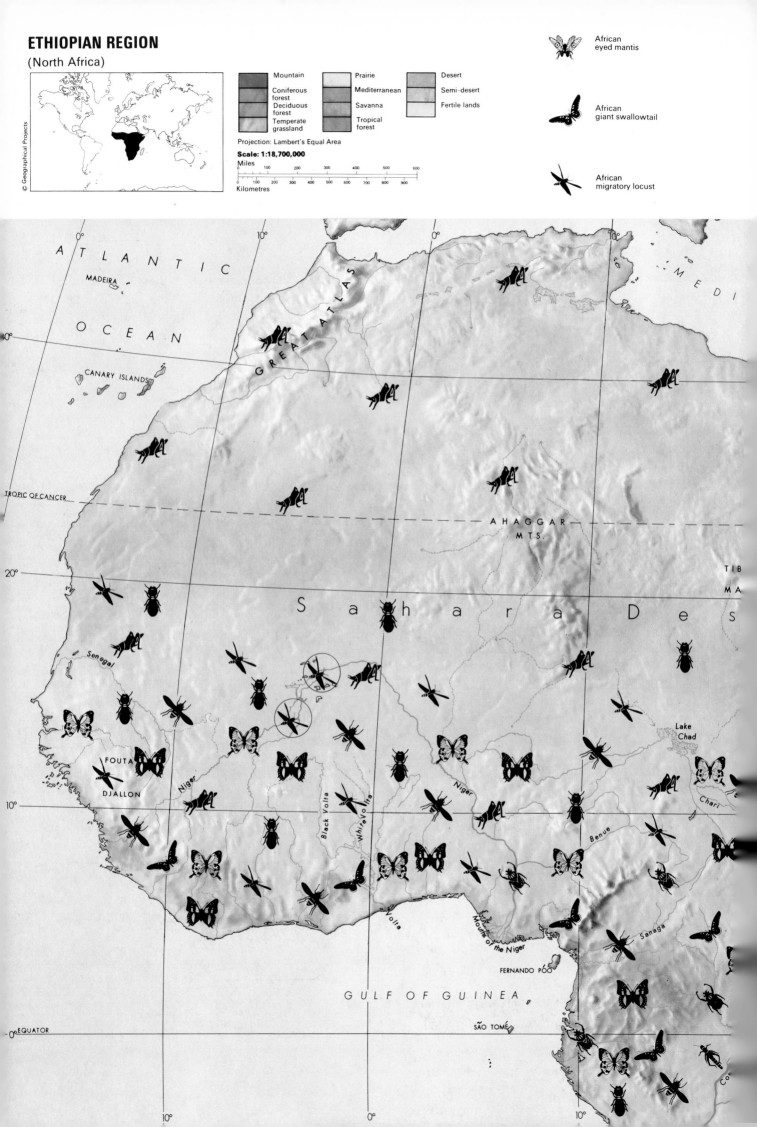

© Geographical Projects

Mountain
Coniferous forest
Deciduous forest
Temperate grassland

Prairie
Mediterranean
Savanna
Tropical forest

Desert
Semi-desert
Fertile lands

Projection: Lambert's Equal Area

Scale: 1:18,700,000

Miles
100   200   300   400   500   600

Kilometres
100   200   300   400   500   600   700   800   900

African eyed mantis

African giant swallowtail

African migratory locust

ATLANTIC OCEAN

MADEIRA

CANARY ISLANDS

GREAT ATLAS

MEDI

TROPIC OF CANCER

AHAGGAR MTS.

20°

TIB MA

S a h a r a   D e s

Senegal

FOUTA DJALLON

Niger

Black Volta

White Volta

Niger

Lake Chad

Chari

Benue

Sanaga

Volta

Mouths of the Niger

FERNANDO PÓO

GULF OF GUINEA

SÃO TOMÉ

EQUATOR

Co

10°

0°

10°

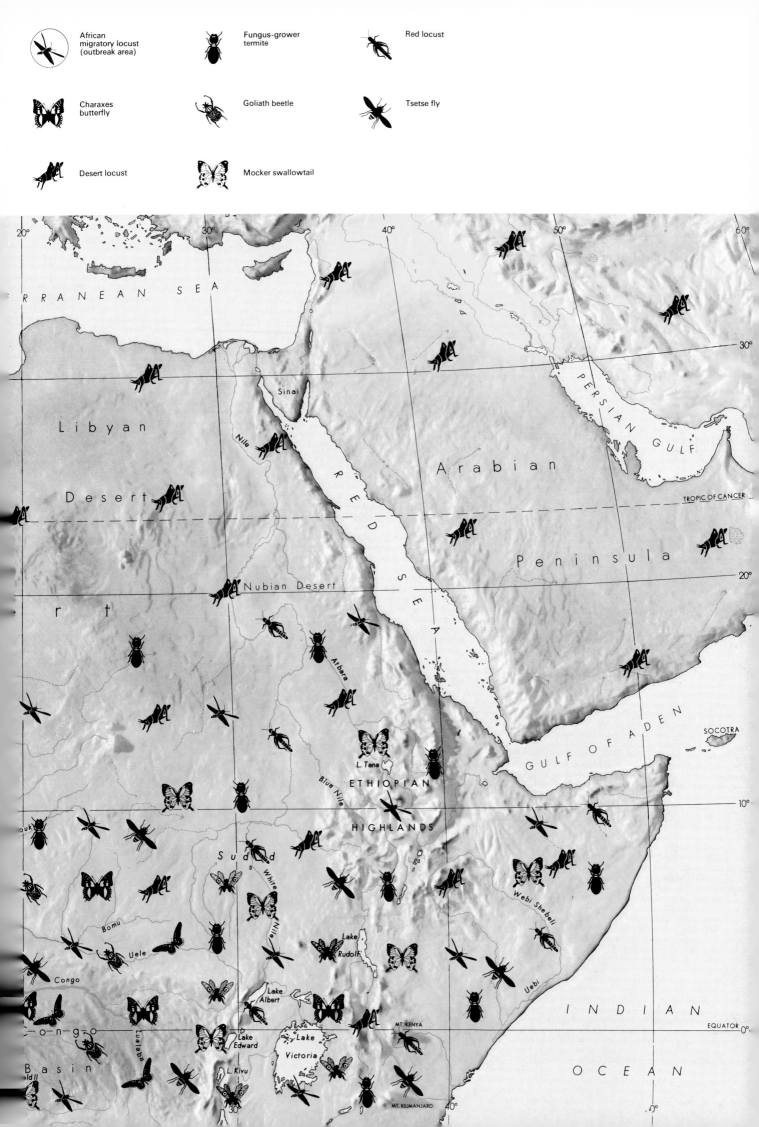

African
migratory locust
(outbreak area)

Fungus-grower
termite

Red locust

Charaxes
butterfly

Goliath beetle

Tsetse fly

Desert locust

Mocker swallowtail

MEDITERRANEAN SEA

20°   30°   40°   50°   60°

Sinai

Nile

RED SEA

Libyan

Desert

Nubian Desert

Atbara

L. Tana

Blue Nile

ETHIOPIAN

HIGHLANDS

Sudd

White Nile

Bomu

Uele

Congo

Lualaba

L. Kivu

Lake
Albert

Lake
Edward

Lake
Victoria

MT. KENYA

MT. KILIMANJARO

Lake
Rudolf

Webi Shebeli

Uebi

Congo

Basin

PERSIAN GULF

Arabian

Peninsula

TROPIC OF CANCER

30°

20°

10°

EQUATOR   0°

GULF OF ADEN

SOCOTRA

INDIAN

OCEAN

0°

30°

captivity the phases can readily be produced by crowding or solitary confinement, and a hopper can even be made to change its phase from one to the other and back again.

In the wild the hoppers tend to become crowded when areas of lush vegetation dry up unevenly, leaving green islands where food is plentiful and in which the insects become concentrated. The next important breakthrough in locust research was the discovery that certain restricted geographical areas, usually the deltas or floodplains of rivers, regularly produce these conditions and form what are called "outbreak areas" for the red and migratory locust. The crowded hoppers give rise to the gregarious-phase locusts, whose instinct is to migrate in closely packed swarms, which breed and multiply much faster than solitary-phase insects. These swarms are the origin of locust plagues.

By identifying the outbreak areas and keeping a constant watch on them the gregarious hoppers can be destroyed before they mature and produce winged swarming locusts in dangerous numbers. By putting this method of control into effect the red locust has been prevented from producing any destructive swarms since 1944 and the African migratory locust since 1948. A number of outbreak areas of the red locust are situated around the great lakes of eastern Africa near and south of the equator. The single important outbreak area of the migratory locust is in the floodplain of the middle Niger in the Republic of Mali.

Termites are found in all tropical regions and extend into the subtropics but not into the cool temperate latitudes. They are present in great variety over the whole of the Ethiopian region and play an important part in the natural ecology and the human economy of Africa. In forest it is the termites that quickly riddle and devour the great trees when they fall, as they are among the very few kinds of animals that can digest wood. Without their services the forest floor would be a deep impenetrable tangle of slowly decaying fallen timber, quite unsuitable for the lives of many of the animals that are naturally at home on the ground in forest. This useful function is generally forgotten when termites are found destroying the timbers of a house or a bridge, which they naturally fail to distinguish from any other dead wood.

In more dry, open country termites play the same part as earthworms do in temperate climates. They burrow in the soil and return to it great quantities of organic matter, thus enhancing its fertility.

In their relations with man termites do immense damage to structural timber and also cause other problems. Some species, for example, make very large above-ground nests, and when ground is being cleared these may be difficult to remove. Sometimes charges of dynamite are required to clear them, as the clay of which the nests are made is cemented with the termites' secretions and is extremely hard.

For an insight into the lives of termites we cannot do better than turn to a harmless and obscure species called the black-mound termite that feeds only on soft decayed wood and other

74

vegetation. It has been closely studied in the Cape region of South Africa by Dr. S. H. Skaife. The nests are hemispherical in shape, black, and about two feet in diameter, projecting from the soil in the form of mounds. They are very hard and are constructed of soil particles cemented with the termites' excrement. In the nest everything, including dead termites and all cast-off skins, is eaten, excreted, and eaten again, passing through the bodies of numbers of individuals until all nourishment is extracted and only a blackish, sticky paste remains. This is used for making the nest so that nothing is wasted and no problem of hygiene arises. If the nest is broken open its interior looks like a large sponge with many irregular cells or cavities communicating with each other by holes just big enough for the termites to creep through.

The inhabitants are all fully formed termites of various sizes, from tiny hatchlings to grown insects; there are no grubs or larvae and no pupae, such as are present in an ants' nest. Here we see one of the fundamental differences between ants and termites. Ants are relatives of bees and wasps and pass through larva and pupa stages; termites are primitive insects with no metamorphosis. They are placed in a distinct order of their own, the Isoptera, and are related to cockroaches, whose young also grow up gradually without the profound changes of form that accompany the growth of the higher insects such as butterflies, beetles, bees, and ants.

As in an ants' nest the great majority of the inhabitants of a termites' nest are workers that play no part in reproduction; but close inspection reveals here again an important difference between ants and termites. The workers in an ants' nest (and those of social bees and wasps) are all sterile females. In the termites' nest they are also sterile, but are of both sexes. Some of the workers have larger jaws than the rest and are often called "soldiers." They defend the nest against enemies, especially ants, and are fed by the ordinary workers.

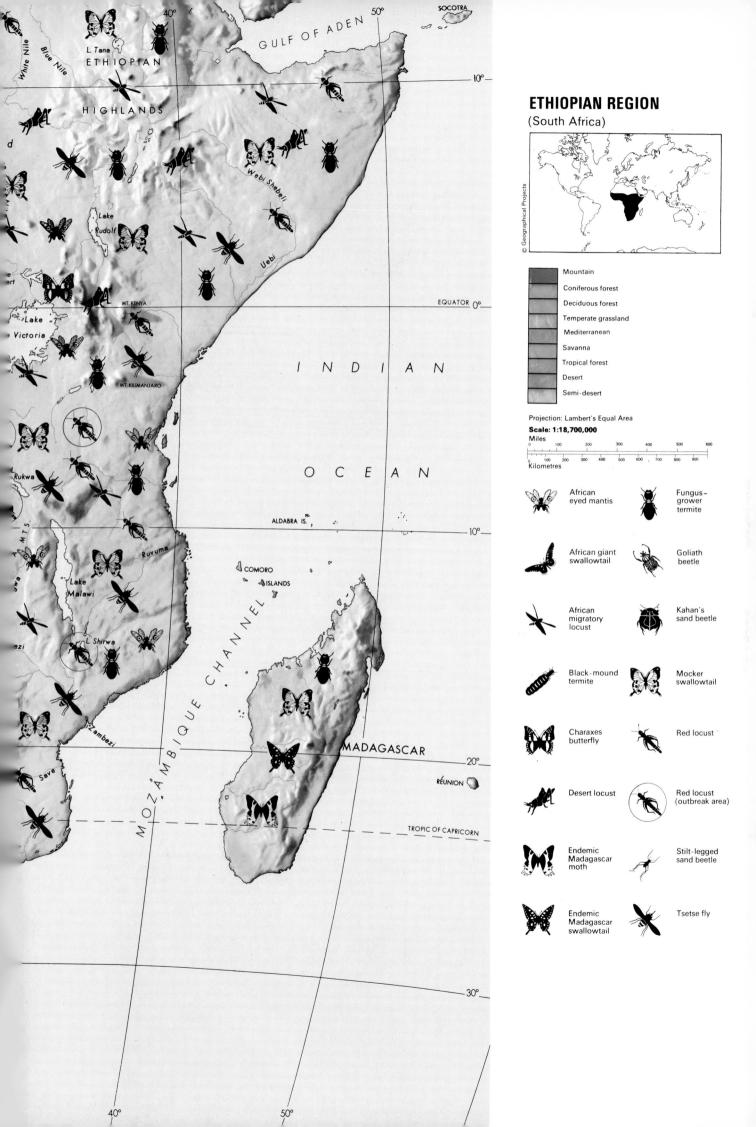

In each nest there is a single queen who may live to an age of 15 years and continues to grow slowly during most of her life. At full size she is three-quarters of an inch long, the workers and soldiers being about one-fifth of an inch. Here is yet another difference from the economy of an ants' nest. The queen ant, like that of the bees and wasps, mates once outside the nest, after which the male dies. The queen termite is accompanied by a consort or "king," a little larger than the workers, who lives with her permanently, mating with her at intervals. The king and queen are constantly fed on predigested food from the mouths of the workers.

The workers are blind and never grow wings, but from time to time winged individuals of both sexes, possessing eyes, are produced and fly away from the nest. When they come to the ground they break off their wings (just as queen ants do) and mate, and new colonies are founded by the very few pairs that survive the attentions of birds and other insectivorous animals.

When alarmed or molested the African eyed mantis faces its enemy and suddenly raises its fore-wings, each of which bears an eye-like spot. The effect is to produce a "face," rather like that of a cat or an owl, and this is thought to have an intimidating effect on birds intending to make a meal of the insect. They are shown here at about twice actual size.

The great majority of the beautiful charaxes butterflies live in Africa, over 80 species of the genus being found in this continent. They have very powerful flight, and the only way to catch them is by luring them with a bait of over-ripe fruit. The white-barred charaxes, shown here, is a fairly common species.

The Namib Desert of south-western Africa is one of the oldest deserts in the world and many of the insects living there are highly adapted for life in sand dunes. Kahan's sand beetle (right) and the stilt-legged sand beetle (left) are specialized for burrowing and for running on the sand, and are found only in this region. They are shown at about twice actual size.

The large fungus-grower is a much more widely spread species of termite that is found all over the warmer parts of Africa in areas of moderate rainfall. It makes large nests, often over six feet high, either conical or with irregular vertical pinnacles and extremely difficult to knock down. Its inhabitants are organized in the way already described with workers and soldiers of both sexes and a king and queen, respectively an inch and up to four inches long. The couple live in a large "royal cell" near the centre of the nest. Wood is the main food of the workers but it is only partly digested and the excrement is collected into spongy heaps inside the nest. On these manure beds a kind of fungus grows which produces tiny white spheres that form the food of the young termites.

The parallel between the fungus-growing termites of the Ethiopian region and the leaf-cutting ants of the Neotropical region is a remarkable special feature of the convergent evolution that has brought about all the similarities between ants and termites.

The African eyed mantis affords a wonderful example of self protection by an intimidating display. When at rest it looks much like an ordinary praying mantis, except that the forewing, which is laid over and conceals its counterpart on the other side, is ornamented with a circular eye-like marking. If the insect is disturbed or threatened it turns and faces its enemy and at the same time suddenly raises the wings, displaying both eye-like markings in such a way as to simulate a "face." This has the effect of startling birds and small insectivorous reptiles and mammals, and in some cases must frighten them enough to dissuade them from attacking.

The Goliath beetle of western tropical Africa is possibly the bulkiest and heaviest insect in the world. Even so, its body is only four inches long and it weighs barely two ounces. This

highlights one of the most noticeable things about insects, which is that in spite of their amazing diversity they never exceed a fairly large mouse in size. Probably the most important reason for this limitation is the insects' mode of breathing. Oxygen is not carried to their tissues and organs by a rapidly circulating blood stream, as it is in vertebrate animals. Instead, air is conveyed to all parts of their bodies by tubes that open along the sides of the body and divide into numerous fine branches inside. The gases of respiration pass into and out of these tubes mainly by diffusion, and this is only adequate to carry them, in such very narrow channels, a distance of about half-an-inch. Thus no part of an insect's body can be more than half-an-inch or so from its outer surface for adequate diffusion to occur.

Some of the most curious of African beetles are to be found in the Namib Desert, which forms a strip of extremely dry territory

Madagascar has been isolated from Africa for at least 60 million years. The island's butterflies are mainly African in origin, their ancestors having come across the sea.

along the entire Atlantic coast of south-western Africa. The Namib is one of the oldest deserts in the world and it harbours many forms of life that have, in the course of long ages of evolution, become adapted in various ways to life in desert sand dunes. The most diverse and numerous of these are beetles of the family Tenebrionidae. There are over 200 species in the Namib, almost all of them found there and nowhere else. Some are fairly normal-looking beetles, but the stilt-legged sand beetles look rather like spiders. They are active in the heat of the day and their very long legs raise them above the level of the hot sand. Kahan's sand beetle is flattened with sharp edges and broad, strong legs. It is nocturnal and burrows in the day time. If exposed to the light these beetles disappear with amazing speed, seeming almost to swim downwards through the loose sand.

Many of the Ethiopian butterflies and moths recall those of the Oriental region and a number of species occur in both regions. These include the African monarch butterfly (a Danaid known in Asia as the plain tiger) and the diadem, whose female mimics the poisonous Danaid monarch just as it does in Asia. The fruit-sucking moth is also common to both regions and there are leaf butterflies and swallowtails allied to the Oriental kinds. Among the butterflies peculiar to the Ethiopian region are almost all the known species of a family called the Acraeidae, which are inedible like the Danaidae and comprise small, narrow-winged butterflies, mostly black-and-orange or black-and-white. They are, as one would expect, mimicked by various species of other families that have no unpalatable qualities. The thick-bodied, powerful, and beautiful butterflies of the genus *Charaxes* have their headquarters in Africa with over 80 species. Only a few of them are found in the Oriental region

The Madagascar clubtail belongs to the swallowtail family of butterflies. It is one of several Madagascar species that show an affinity with the fauna of Asia rather than Africa.

and one is found in southern Europe. They fly very strongly and are hard to catch, but can be attracted to a bait of rotten fruit such as banana or pineapple.

Africa's largest and finest butterfly is a swallowtail, aptly called the African giant swallowtail. It rivals in size the great birdwing swallowtails of the Australian tropics, but differs by the male, not the female, being the larger. Males of the African species range up to nine inches in wing-span and have long, narrow fore-wings. The females span only six inches. The African giant swallowtail is found in the rain forest of West Africa and Zaire where it inhabits the forest canopy. Males come down to drink at muddy places by forest pools, but the smaller females are very seldom seen and not more than half-a-dozen have ever been collected. The early stages are unknown.

One of the most remarkable butterflies of the region, or indeed of the world, is the mocker swallowtail. In what is evidently its primitive form it is a typical swallowtail butterfly, pale yellow and black with tails on the hind-wings, and in Madagascar and Ethiopia both sexes have this appearance. In other parts of Africa, however, the females are always mimics of one inedible butterfly or another. In some places all the mocker swallowtail females closely resemble the African monarch, just as females of the diadem butterfly do. In other places they are all marked with black and white and are hardly distinguishable from a Danaid species called the friar. Sometimes these two forms fly together. None of these mimetic females look anything like a typical swallowtail and all of them lack tails on the hind-wing. And yet the males bred from their eggs are always tailed and black-and-yellow, and the larvae and pupae are, of course, of the normal swallowtail type.

The day-flying moth Chrysiridia madagascarensis *has been called "the most magnificent living creature." Its glowing colours are "structural," depending on interference effects, not on pigments, and they change with varying incidence of the light. Its nearest relatives are the* Urania *moths of tropical America, and its presence in Madagascar is a geographical mystery.*

The African giant swallowtail is the largest butterfly found in the continent, and one of the largest in the world. It lives in the rain forests of western Africa and Zaire (the Congo) and males can occasionally be seen drinking, with other butterflies, beside muddy pools. Females, which are smaller than males, are very seldom seen, and probably live permanently high up in the forest canopy.

We have mentioned that a non-mimetic and probably primitive form of the mocker swallowtail lives in Madagascar. This large island, together with the Comoro islands, the Mascarenes, and the Seychelles, comprises a distinct subregion within the Ethiopian region known as the Malagasy subregion. Its remarkable fauna of lemurs and recently extinct giant birds is well known and its butterflies are also of interest. Madagascar became isolated from Africa at least 60 million years ago, probably before butterflies as we know them had evolved. The ancestors of all the butterflies now living in this subregion must, therefore, have come from across the sea. Most of them have been there long enough to evolve into distinct species. Of the 301 species of Malagasy butterflies 233 are endemic, that is, wholly confined to the area. As one would expect, most of them are clearly of African origin, but two Asian types, wholly absent from Africa, are found there. These comprise five species of the genus *Euploea* (of the Danaid family), which are abundant in Asia and known as "crows," and one species of *Atrophaneura*, a kind of swallowtail, which we can call the Madagascar clubtail from the shape of the tail on its hind-wing. In common with its Asian relatives the larvae of the Madagascar clubtail feed on poisonous creepers of the genus *Aristolochia*, and the poison is retained by the insects, both larvae and butterflies, rendering them inedible. Here is a swallowtail that is protected, not by mimicking other butterflies but by having inedible properties and a distinctive appearance of its own.

The presence of Asian types of butterflies in Malagasy is remarkable, but that of the beautiful moth *Chrysiridia madagascarensis* is even more anomalous, for its nearest relatives are the Urania moths of the Neotropical region. Possibly these moths were widespread in the past but have become extinct in all but these two widely separated regions.

6 The Neotropical Region

The tropical part of Mexico, and Central and South America. The islands of the West Indies are included here, although they can be considered as a separate island region.

In spite of its name this region extends southward considerably beyond the tropics, but it lies within them from its northern limit in Mexico to Bolivia, Paraguay, and southern Brazil in the south. The great tropical archipelago of the West Indies is included in the region. The enormous catchment basin of the Amazon River in Brazil, Colombia, Peru, and Bolivia forms the largest continuous area of tropical rain forest in the world, and it is here that the highly characteristic Neotropical insect fauna is found in its greatest richness and diversity.

South and Central America existed through a long period of geological time as an island continent, cut off from the great land masses to the north just as Australia has been up to the present time. Both vegetation and insect life have developed far more luxuriantly in South America than in Australia, however, owing to the much higher rainfall over most of the continent.

The butterflies of South and Central America and the West Indies are, taken as a whole, the most splendid and diverse of any region of the world and several entire families are almost confined to the Neotropical region. The most famous of these is the Morphidae, or morphos, whose shining blue wings were at one time used extensively to make ornaments and jewelry, the butterflies being bred commercially for the purpose in Brazil. Most of them are large, with a wing-span of five or six inches, and one species, *Morpho hecuba*, spans seven inches and is the largest butterfly of the New World. Only the male morphos have the vivid iridescent blue coloration, the females being usually orange or brown. *M. hecuba* is usually tawny or dark brown in both sexes, but a lavender blue variety is found in the lower Amazon. Morpho larvae are covered with poisonous stinging hairs and live gregariously in a communal web in which they also pupate.

The great owlet moth has a wider wing expanse than any other butterfly or moth. It flies by night in the tropical American forests, and by day rests on trees where its mottled grey pattern makes it hard to see. It is shown here at actual size.

NEOTROPICAL REGION
(Mexico & Central America)

© Geographical Projects

Mountain	Prairie	Semi-desert
Coniferous forest	Savanna	
Deciduous forest	Tropical forest	
Temperate grassland	Desert	

Projection: Lambert's Equal Area

Scale: 1:14,300,000

Miles
0   100   200   300   400

Kilometres
0   100   200   300   400   500   600   700

Ancyluris formosissima

Army ant

Beechey's bee

Colorado

Gila

Lower California

GULF OF CALIFORNIA

110°

Rio Grande

SIERRA MADRE OCCIDENTAL

100°

Brazos

Red

Mississippi

90°

30°

TROPIC OF CANCER

Rio Grande

SIERRA MADRE ORIENTAL

Missi Del

GULF

M E X I

Rio Grande de Santiago

20°

GULF OF CAMPECHE

SIERRA MADRE DEL SUR

Isthmus of Tehuantepec

Yu

0°

P A C I F I C   O C E A N

110°

100°

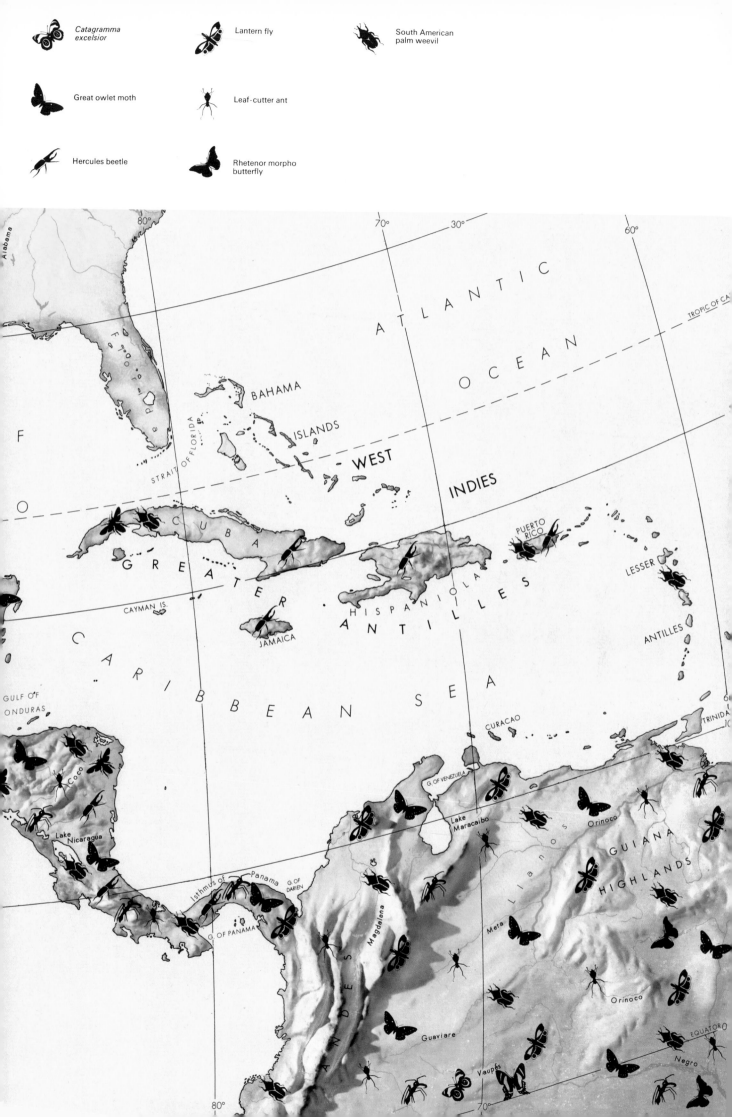

Catagramma
excelsior

Lantern fly

South American
palm weevil

Great owlet moth

Leaf-cutter ant

Hercules beetle

Rhetenor morpho
butterfly

ATLANTIC

OCEAN

TROPIC OF CA

F

BAHAMA

ISLANDS

WEST

INDIES

O

STRAIT OF FLORIDA

C U B A

G R E A T E R

PUERTO
RICO

CAYMAN IS.

A N T I L L E S

LESSER

JAMAICA

HISPANIOLA

ANTILLES

C

CARIBBEAN SEA

GULF OF
ONDURAS

CURACAO

TRINIDA

G. OF VENEZUELA

Lake
Maracaibo

Orinoco

Coco

GUIANA

Lake
Nicaragua

L l a n o s

Isthmus of Panama

G. OF
DARIEN

HIGHLANDS

Meta

Magdalena

G. OF PANAMA

Orinoco

EQUATOR O

Guaviare

Negro

Vaupés

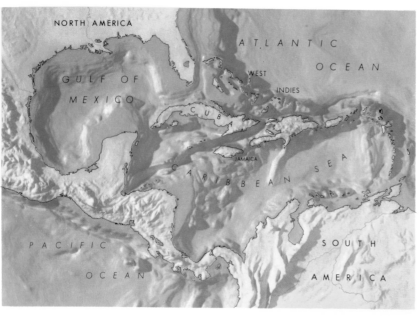

The rhetenor morpho *illustrates well the great difference between the males and females of these splendid butterflies. Only the males exhibit the brilliant blue colour that has made them famous.*

The sardanapalus butterfly is one of the most beautiful species of the genus Agrias. It flies in the Amazonian forests and is not rare, but its powerful flight makes it difficult to catch.

Map above: As far as insect distribution is concerned the West Indies are considered as part of the Neotropical region, their insects being largely shared with the mainland of Central and South America. There are some insects confined to the islands, however, including a swallowtail butterfly found only on Jamaica.

Here are two more butterflies chosen to represent the marvellously rich and beautiful assemblage of these insects that fly in the South American rain forest. Ancyluris formosissima (bottom) is unusual in having its brilliant pattern developed on both upper- and undersides of the wings. Catagramma excelsior (top) belongs to a genus in which the underside of the hind-wings is beautifully patterned.

The Brassolidae, or owl butterflies, are also exclusively Neotropical. They are large and not usually brightly coloured, their most characteristic feature being a large eye-like spot on the underside of each hind-wing. By flicking the wings open the insect displays both spots together and the resultant simulation of the face of an owl may be effective in scaring away enemies.

The Ithomiidae and Heliconiidae are the other two important families that are almost confined to the Neotropical region. Anatomically they are distinct, but they are rather similar in appearance, with long, narrow fore-wings and slender bodies. Like the Danaidae, they are all protected by having inedible qualities, and many are involved in mimicry associations of quite bewildering complexity. Not only do butterflies belonging to edible groups resemble them in appearance, but they, and some of the Neotropical Danaids as well, resemble each other, so that several species of all three distasteful families have come to look so alike that careful examination is needed to separate them.

The purpose of this sort of mimicry is not immediately apparent, but it can be explained by the reasonable assumption that birds have to learn by experience which butterflies are good to eat and which are poisonous or nasty. Every young insectivorous bird is likely to attack and injure a number of inedible butterflies with warning coloration before it learns to leave them alone. If numerous patterns and colour schemes had to be learned a great many inedible butterflies would be attacked by a bird in the course of its gastronomic education, and it might continue to make mistakes throughout its life. By "clubbing together" to display a few distinctive patterns the different families of inedible butterflies must certainly reduce the total incidence of attack by inexperienced birds.

The simple form of mimicry by edible butterflies of ill-tasting ones was first demonstrated by an English naturalist, H. W. Bates; the more subtle mimicry of each other by inedible ones was discovered by the German, W. Müller, and they are called Batesian and Müllerian mimicry accordingly. Both of these naturalists worked on butterflies of the Amazon basin.

The Heliconiid butterflies have the curious habit of "roosting" night after night in closely packed crowds in a particular tree or bush. Nocturnal predators cannot see warning colours, but they can probably detect the unpleasant smell of a mass of sleeping butterflies and learn to leave them alone.

In addition to these endemic families almost all the more widely spread groups of butterflies are lavishly represented in the American tropics, many of the species being wonderfully coloured and patterned.

Little can be said here of the equally wonderful assemblage of moths found in the Neotropical forests. One of these, however, must be mentioned. This is the great owlet, which in one sense, is the largest moth in the world, for it has a wing expanse that sometimes exceeds 12 inches. The Hercules moth of tropical Australia has a greater wing area, and some of the largest hawk-moths are certainly heavier. Which is in fact the biggest of them is a matter that readers must decide for themselves.

In the temperate and cold parts of South America butterflies and moths, and indeed all insects, are far less numerous, but one group of butterflies inhabiting this region is of interest. Clouded yellows (genus *Colias*) are found extending even to the cold, stormy island of Tierra del Fuego. They are characteristic butterflies of the Palaearctic and Nearctic regions and their presence in southern Chile and Argentina can only be explained by supposing that the cool climate of the high Andes has provided them with a migratory route from the north. This supposition

From top to bottom: Heliconius eurate, Mechanitis lysimnia, Lycorea halia. *These three South American butterflies belong to three distinct families, the Heliconiidae, Ithomiidae, and Danaidae respectively, and so are not closely related to each other. However they have two characteristics in common, an obvious similarity in appearance and the property of being distasteful to birds. This is a case of mimicry differing from that illustrated on pages 63 and 80 because here the species which mimic each other are all nasty-tasting and inedible.*

The clouded yellow butterflies of the genus Colias *are widespread in the cold and temperate parts of the Old and New Worlds. Vauthier's clouded yellow is found in southern South America.*

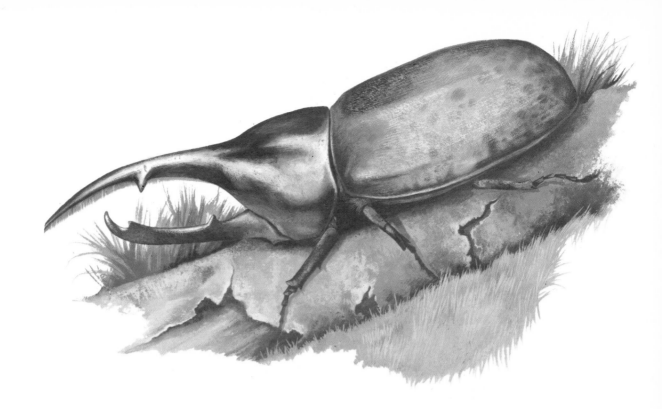

The Hercules beetle is a rival of the African Goliath beetle (page 69) for the distinction of being the world's bulkiest insect. The grotesque horns on head and thorax are found only in males.

is supported by the occurrence of a number of species of *Colias* along the Andean chain. Vauthier's clouded yellow is the most widespread of the southern species.

From the butterflies and moths of the Neotropical region we turn now to other groups of insects. The huge beetles of the genus *Dynastes* are very characteristic of the Neotropical region, though some of the smaller species are found to the north of the region. The Hercules beetle of the West Indies and Central America is probably the largest of all of them. The male may be six inches long, of which over two inches is accounted for by the upper one of the two horns that project in front. This is a prolongation of the thorax, the lower horn being a prolongation of the head. By up-and-down movements of the head the two horns can be worked like a pair of forceps.

The horns are present only in the males and their function is by no means clear. If two males are put together they usually fight, each trying to pick the other up bodily and slam it down again. The loser in these battles seems to suffer little harm. Although smaller individuals are always defeated, they are just as successful as big ones in mating with females when a number of beetles are confined together. Large males have been seen to pick a female up and carry her off bodily, but this is not an essential prelude to mating. The horns appear to be ineffective as defensive weapons against possible enemies.

Another giant among the beetles is the South American palm weevil, which is about one-and-a-half-inches long. Most weevils (over 40,000 species are known) are small or minute insects, but the palm weevils, various species of which occur all round the tropics, are unusually large. The South American palm weevil is a coal-black, hard-shelled beetle that lays its eggs in the soft tissues of various kinds of palm trees. In early times it was a useful animal as it infested only wild palms and the big white grubs were eaten by the native people. Under the name "gru-gru worms" they are still used as food in some parts of the region.

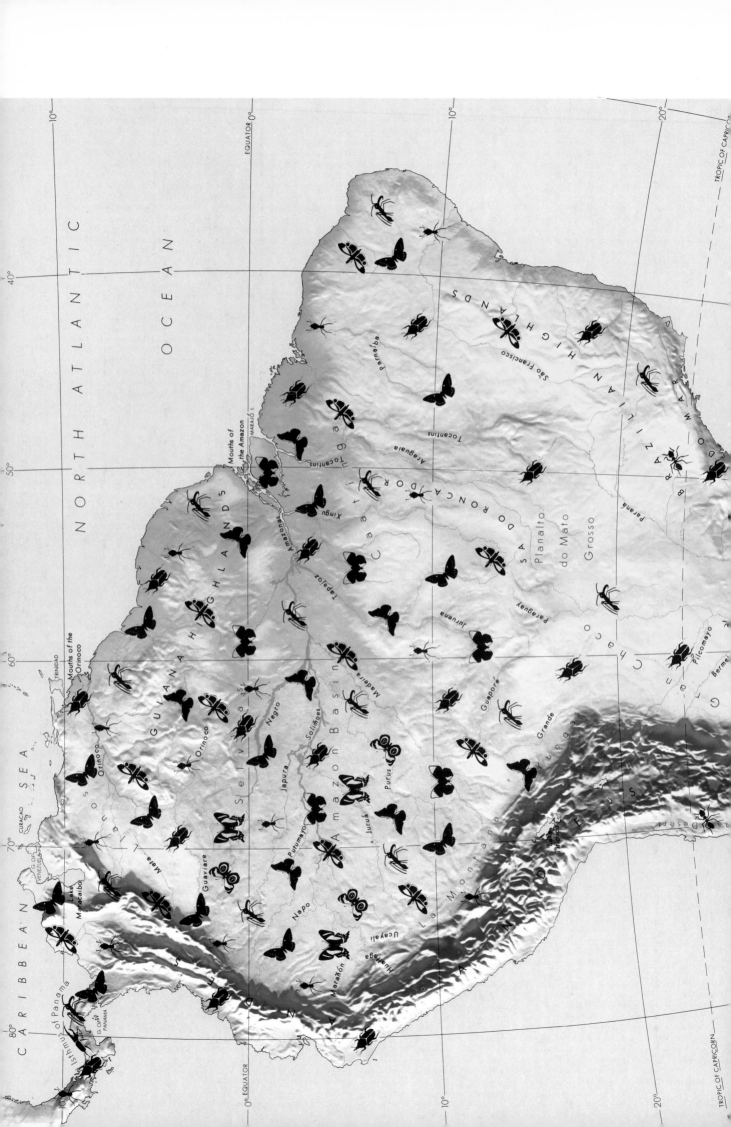

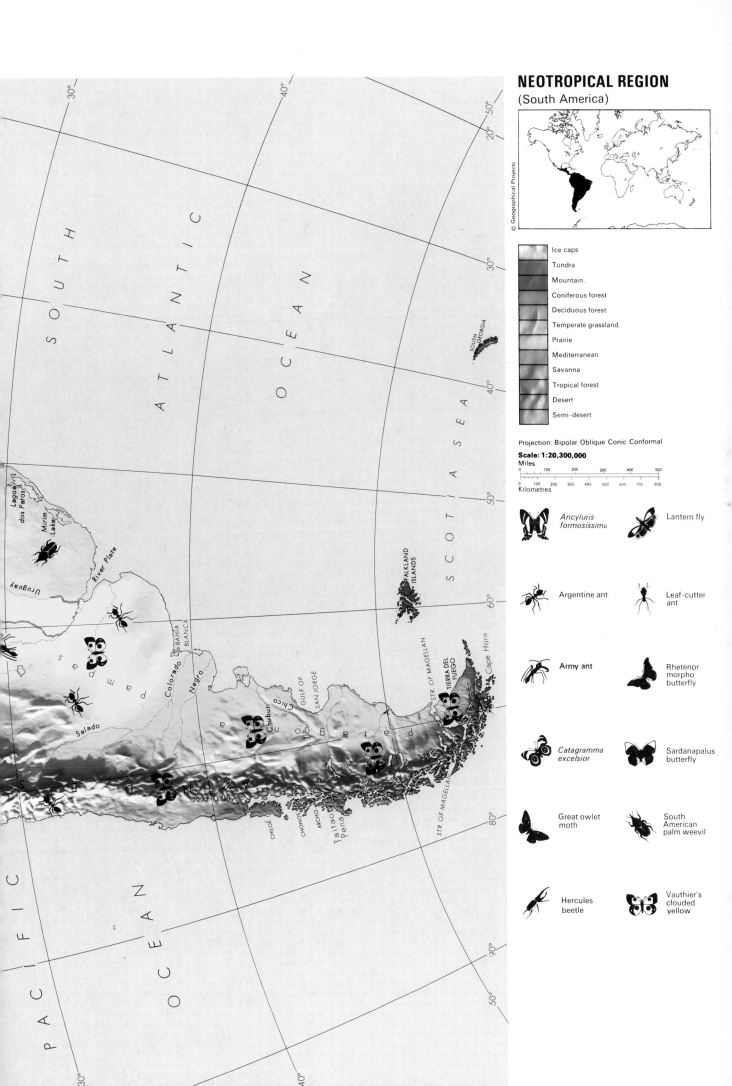

With the introduction and cultivation of the coconut palm the status of the weevil changed to that of a serious pest. The larvae eat out galleries in the heart of the plant, the so-called "palm cabbage," causing the top of the tree to fall over. This is the first sign of infestation and the tree dies soon afterwards. Related species of palm weevils are found in the tropical parts of Asia and Africa and some of these have red markings on the thorax. All attack palms, both the coconut and the African oil palm, and they are very difficult to control.

All tropical rain forests teem with ants of numerous kinds, and they are nowhere more abundant and conspicuous than in the Neotropical jungle. The most noticeable of them are the leaf-cutter ants, which are almost confined to the region, one species occurring just to the north in Texas. The workers can often be seen marching on the ground or along twigs and branches, many individuals carrying pieces of leaf cut from the foliage of a nearby tree or bush. Their burdens make them conspicuous and have led to their being fancifully called "parasol ants."

They nest in enormous colonies that have tunnels and galleries extending underground to a depth of 10 feet and to a radius of 100 feet or more. Each colony has a population of about half a million ants. The workers are remarkable in being differentiated into numerous types, from big "soldiers" to tiny "gardeners," the leaf collecting being done by grades of intermediate size. The pieces of leaf are carried down into the nest, but are not used directly as food. They are chewed up to form a compost on which a particular kind of fungus is cultivated. Nothing else is allowed to grow in the fungus beds, and they are tended and pruned so that rounded knobs called bromatia are produced, these forming the sole food of the ants. If grown in the absence of the ants the fungi never produce bromatia. Each species of leaf-cutter ant always cultivates a particular fungus species, though the same kind of fungus may be used by more than one species of ant. When the queen leaf-cutters fly away to found new colonies they carry, in a pouch below the mouth, a scrap of fungus from which a new culture can be started. These ants are a serious pest in coffee plantations and citrus orchards, as they defoliate trees as a source of leaf-mould.

The other conspicuous ants are the army ants of the genus *Eciton*. They are hunters that rove in swarms numbering from 1 to 2 million. Unlike other ants they have no fixed home or

Leaf-cutter ants are shown here cutting out pieces of leaves and carrying them away. They do not eat the leaves but use them to make a compost on which they cultivate a fungus that provides them with food.

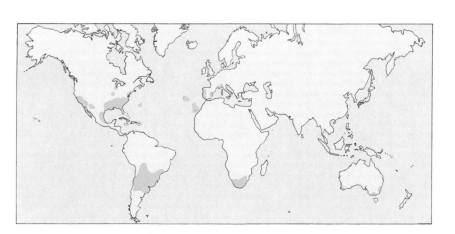

This map shows the world-wide distribution of the Argentine ant. It has spread rapidly from its home in South America and attacks native ants, as well as other insects and animals, in many parts of the world. In the homes and gardens of Cape Town, for example, only the Argentine ant can be found today; formerly they harboured many harmless native African species of ants.

Although it is not a very large beetle, the South American palm weevil is a giant among the weevils, most of which are small or minute. It is a serious pest of the coconut palm.

Army ants are nomads, and do not inhabit permanent nests or colonies, but roam the forest floor, camping at intervals to complete their breeding cycle. There may be a million individuals in a single swarm.

"nest" but are nomadic, operating from temporary bivouacs, which are of two distinct kinds, depending on the stages of the ants' breeding cycle. When the queen is engaged in laying eggs the ants camp for about three weeks inside a hollow log from which they raid on a fairly small scale. At this stage the individuals of the previous cycle are pupae, and these hatch in the secure shelter of the static bivouac. As soon as they are all hatched into ants, the queen ceases laying and the whole swarm leaves the bivouac, carrying with it the young larvae that have hatched from the recently laid eggs. While the larvae are growing and in need of abundant food, temporary bivouacs are made under, not inside, logs, and the ants camp in them for only a day or two before moving on. During this phase, which lasts about two weeks, they hunt ceaselessly, destroying enormous numbers of other insects. As soon as the larvae are fully grown and ready to pupate the cycle starts over again with renewed egg-laying in a new static bivouac.

The notorious Argentine ant is anything but conspicuous, but it has been named "the most pernicious ant in the world." This tiny insect, native to subtropical South America, was first col-

lected near Buenos Aires in 1866. Nothing more was heard of it for 25 years, when it was reported in New Orleans, apparently having been brought there by ships trading with South America. It spread rapidly in the southern United States and was carried across the Atlantic Ocean to Madeira and Portugal by 1907, and to Cape Town in 1908. Between about 1940 and 1950 it reached Melbourne, Perth, and Sydney in Australia, and it has spread widely in southern Europe.

Clearly the Argentine ant is one of those insects whose natural ecology has fitted it to be a commensal of man, though it cannot establish itself in regions with even fairly severe winters or in fully tropical climates. In houses it is a nuisance and very difficult to get rid of. Out of doors it attacks sitting hens and young chicks and invades beehives. In orchards it encourages harmful plant lice and aphids by driving off their natural enemies. To the native ants of any region it reaches it is like a science fiction invader from outer space; it attacks and exterminates them.

To speak of a stingless bee seems almost a contradiction in terms, but there is a large family of social bees, the Meliponidae, in which the sting is vestigial and useless as a weapon. They are found in the tropics and subtropics around the world, but the genus *Melipona* is confined to the Neotropical region. Most of them nest in hollow trees or branches, and at the entrance a tube or spout of wax is made, possibly to guide the bees home.

There are queens, males, or drones, and workers, as in other social bees, and honey is stored in the same way in parts of the comb not used for breeding. The grubs are not fed by the workers, however, as they are by those of the honeybee. In a nest of stingless bees each brood cell is filled with pollen and honey, furnished with an egg by the queen and then sealed up, so that there is no contact between the adult and the larvae. There is therefore no opportunity for the special feeding from the pharyngeal glands of the workers that causes a female larva to develop into a queen, rather than a worker, in a honeybee colony. In *Melipona* there is no difference in size between the

When Columbus landed in Cuba, one of his earliest landfalls in the New World, he was given honey to eat. This was produced by a domesticated species of bee, Beechey's bee, quite distinct from the familiar honeybee and differing in not possessing a sting. This small stingless bee has been kept from early historical times both on the West Indian islands and on the mainland of Central America. The bee in the foreground is shown larger than actual size.

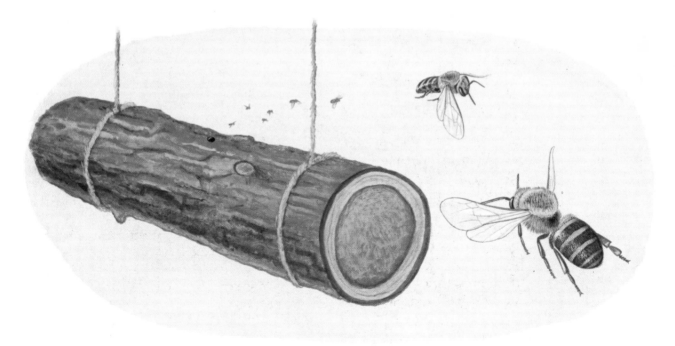

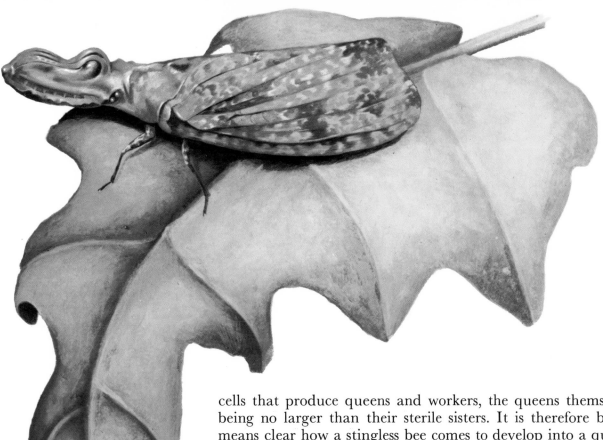

The tropical American lantern fly is a remarkable insect, but it is not luminous, as its name suggests. The hollow forward prolongation of the head has markings which call to mind the head of an alligator on a minute scale. It is possible that its reptilian appearance serves to scare off insectivorous birds.

cells that produce queens and workers, the queens themselves being no larger than their sterile sisters. It is therefore by no means clear how a stingless bee comes to develop into a queen. It seems likely that this depends not on her diet as a larva but on her hereditary constitution, and a rather complicated genetical system has been worked out to explain the facts.

In his report on Cuba, one of the earliest landfalls in the New World, Columbus noted a kind of honey as one of the island's assets. This was almost certainly the product of Beechey's bee, a species of *Melipona*, which had been domesticated on the mainland by the Maya Indians of Mexico from early historical times. The bees are accommodated in hollow logs two or three feet long that are plugged at each end with clay and have a flight hole bored into the central cavity about halfway along. These are hung up horizontally, or placed on scaffolding, and may be occupied naturally by a swarm or provided with a portion of brood comb and a handful of bees from an occupied hive. Since they cannot sting the bees can actually be taken up by handfuls. To harvest the honey one clay plug is removed and the nearest honey comb taken out.

The so-called lantern fly, which is found in the forests from Panama southward through Brazil to Bolivia, was given this name and the zoological name *Laternaria* under the mistaken belief that it is luminous in life. In common with some other members of the family Fulgoridae it has the front part of the head prolonged into a hollow structure, which in this case bears markings that give the insect an extraordinary and quite alarming appearance. Low down on each side a curved line of alternating dark and light rectangles simulates a grinning mouthful of teeth, and marks like an eye and a nostril complete the resemblance, on a very small scale, to the head of an alligator. It cannot be supposed that it derives protection from this particular resemblance, but the simulation of a reptilian face of any kind is enough to put the horrifying thought of snakes into the head of any searching bird, just as the Oriental caterpillar shown on page 66 almost certainly does.

7 The Australian Region

New Guinea and the neighbouring islands, Australia, and Tasmania. Celebes, the Moluccas, and the Lesser Sunda Islands form a transitional zone between the Australian and Oriental regions.

The main components of the Australian region are the continent of Australia, with Tasmania off its southern coast, and the great island of New Guinea to the north of it. Just as the islands of Java, Sumatra, and Borneo stand on an extension of the continental shelf (the Sunda Shelf) from Asia, so do New Guinea and some of the smaller islands near it stand on the Sahul Shelf, an extension from Australia. The Aru Islands are the most important of the small islands on the Sahul Shelf and close by them are the Moluccas, including the islands of Halmahera, Buru, and Serang that lie just off the shelf in slightly deeper water. Together with New Guinea these islands comprise the Papuan subregion of the Australian region. To the east of New Guinea are the islands of the Bismark and Solomon archipelagoes, which have a predominantly Australian fauna and are included in the region.

In the deep water between the Sunda and Sahul shelves lie a large number of islands, Celebes the biggest of them, which have been the subject of much zoogeographical controversy. For our purpose they can be regarded as occupying an area transitional between the Oriental and Australian regions.

There is good evidence that the Australian region has been separated by the ocean from the rest of the continents, except for Antarctica, since some time in the Mesozoic era. As a consequence many archaic types of animals have survived there, which formerly existed on the other continents but became extinct in the face of competition from the more adaptable and efficient animals that evolved on them. The mammals are the best known and most conspicuous of these, including as they do all the living marsupials (except the opossums and rat-opossums of America) and the extraordinary egg-laying mammals, the

Queen Alexandra's birdwing is confined to south-eastern New Guinea. The male is a magnificent insect and the soberly coloured female has the distinction of being the largest butterfly in the world. The butterflies of the genus Ornithoptera are very characteristic of the Papuan subregion.

platypus and echidna. For reasons explained in the first chapter the Australian insect fauna shows a less marked contrast with that of the rest of the world than do most of the vertebrate animals, but there are nevertheless some remarkable "living fossils" among the Australian insects.

When discussing termites in Chapter 5 we mentioned that their nearest relatives, and almost certainly their evolutionary ancestors, are the cockroaches. One Australian species affords ample evidence in confirmation of this theory of the termites' origin. It is quite definitely a termite and lives in large communities, or nests, as all these insects do. Its name is *Mastotermes darwiniensis*, but as it is the only living representative of the genus we can just call it *Mastotermes*.

It displays a remarkable assemblage of primitive, cockroach-like features, including unusually large size in the reproductive individuals ("kings" and "queens"), whose wings may span as much as two inches. The hind-wing has a distinct lobe on its hind margin, recalling the condition in cockroaches, and the egg-laying organ, or ovipositor, of the female is of cockroach type. Cockroaches lay their eggs inside a capsule called an ootheca, the eggs usually being arranged in two rows. *Mastotermes* alone among termites, lay eggs in a similar capsular structure in batches of 24, arranged in two rows of 12. Fossil relatives of *Mastotermes* are known from strata of Eocene age,

The compass termite is not itself a remarkable insect and it belongs to a widely ranging genus not confined to Australia, though its own range is very restricted. The above-ground nests that it makes are extraordinary structures. They are up to 12 feet high and seen on end have the form of narrow wedges. Their really remarkable feature, however, is that they are always accurately orientated so that their sides face east and west. The purpose of this is probably to minimize rapid changes in temperature inside the nest.

Map opposite: The islands that run from Southeast Asia to Australia have never formed a land bridge, but many Asian type butterflies and other insects have reached northern Australia by "island hopping".

50 to 60 million years old. Primitive termites probably existed long before that time, but definitely recognizable fossils of them have yet to be found.

In spite of its ancient lineage *Mastotermes* has by no means the status of a rare and dwindling relic. On the contrary it is a most abundant and destructive insect and ranges widely north of the Tropic of Capricorn, both in coastal and inland districts. Its diet also ranges widely: it attacks structural timber, working so fast that it can destroy a house completely in two or three years, and it also eats various stored products such as paper, flour, hay, and rubber. Living trees, shrubs, and vegetables are attacked, and it is a serious pest of sugar cane. In natural conditions it often hollows out branches and small trees, and the aborigines use these tubular pieces of wood to make a musical instrument called a didgeridoo.

Another most interesting and quite harmless species is the compass termite. It lives on a diet of dry grass and is a member of the same genus, *Amitermes,* as the black-mound termite of South Africa. It has a very limited range, being apparently confined to a 50-mile radius around Darwin, and is remarkable for its large above-ground nests, which are accurately orientated to the points of the compass. The nests are up to 12 feet high and usually a little less in length. Seen on end they have the form of slender wedges, three feet wide at ground level, quickly narrowing to 18 inches, and then gradually to the thin serrated top. Above the broad base one face is slightly convex, the other vertical, and the mounds always stand with the long axis precisely north and south. They are grey in colour and constructed of a sort of cement compounded of soil and the termites' excrement. Almost all the galleries in which the inmates live are just under the surface, with a few passages crossing from one side to the other. The nest is thus formed of a thin outer covering and a solid core, with a spongy layer between them on each side.

It is thought that the purpose of the orientation is to minimize rapid changes in temperature inside the nest. In the morning the sun will shine directly on the east side of the nest; as it rises higher and increases in strength its rays will strike more and more obliquely until noon, when they will cease to be directed onto the sides of the nest at all. In the afternoon and evening

Australia is a land of "living fossils," and one of the most remarkable of these is the primitive termite Mastotermes. In both structure and habits it shows features that strongly support the view that cockroaches are the evolutionary ancestors of termites. Although it is a relict form from the remote past, Mastotermes is by no means a rarity. It is one of the species that damage timber on a serious scale.

101

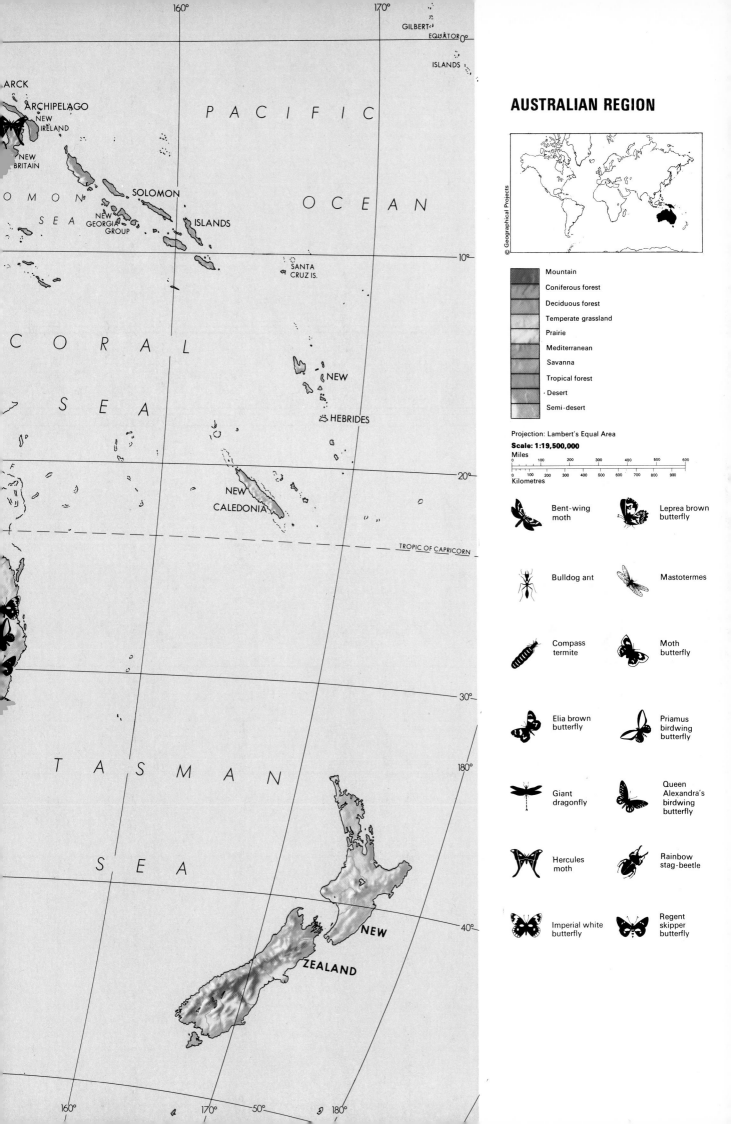

AUSTRALIAN REGION

© Geographical Projects

Mountain
Coniferous forest
Deciduous forest
Temperate grassland
Prairie
Mediterranean
Savanna
Tropical forest
Desert
Semi-desert

Projection: Lambert's Equal Area

Scale: 1:19,500,000

Miles
0   100   200   300   400   500   600

Kilometres
0   100   200   300   400   500   600   700   800   900

Bent-wing moth

Leprea brown butterfly

Bulldog ant

Mastotermes

Compass termite

Moth butterfly

Elia brown butterfly

Priamus birdwing butterfly

Giant dragonfly

Queen Alexandra's birdwing butterfly

Hercules moth

Rainbow stag-beetle

Imperial white butterfly

Regent skipper butterfly

Map labels

EQUATOR 0°

GILBERT ISLANDS

ARCK ARCHIPELAGO
NEW IRELAND
NEW BRITAIN

PACIFIC

OCEAN

OMON SEA

SOLOMON ISLANDS

NEW GEORGIA GROUP

SANTA CRUZ IS.

10°

CORAL SEA

NEW HEBRIDES

20°

NEW CALEDONIA

TROPIC OF CAPRICORN

30°

TASMAN

180°

SEA

NEW ZEALAND

40°

50°

160°   170°   180°

160°   170°

this sequence is repeated in reverse. In cool weather the termites crowd over to the side that is receiving the sun's heat and on hot days they go to the shaded side.

It is interesting to note that some other Australian species of *Amitermes*, which normally make rounded mound nests, construct elongate north-south oriented nests in marshes. When living in dry soil they have a system of underground tunnels below the mound into which they retreat during the heat of the day. In waterlogged soil they cannot do this and so, as an alternative means of escaping the sun's heat, they construct the elongate nests characteristic of the compass termites.

The bulldog ants are well known to all but the most urban of Australians. They are classified in a distinct subfamily, the Myrmecinae, that is entirely confined to Australia and Tasmania. Like *Mastotermes*, bulldog ants have the status of a relic from early geological times when the group was world-wide in distribution. They are large, being an inch or more long, with formidable stings and are often brightly coloured. They make conspicuous nests marked by mounds or craters of excavated earth. They run rapidly and are unusual among ants in having the power to jump for distances of seven or eight inches.

It is in the economy of the nest that these ants display obvious primitive features. One of these is the formation of small colonies numbering from 500 to 2,000 individuals; most higher ants' nests have far more than this. There is usually a single queen, not very different from the workers, and the practice of mouth-to-mouth feeding with regurgitated liquid food is not found. Each ant forages for itself, living mainly on nectar from flowers and collecting insects as food for the larvae. In the nest the insects are simply cut into pieces and fed to the larvae, which are far more active than those of most other ants. Sometimes they will attack and eat each other if food is short. The habit of mouth-to-mouth exchange of food, known as trophallaxis, is so characteristic of the higher ants (and of termites and social bees and wasps as well) that its absence in the bulldog ants is of great

The large aggressive bulldog ants are well known to all rural Australians and their stings are justly feared. They belong to a group of primitive hunting ants, widespread in former geological times, but now confined to Australia.

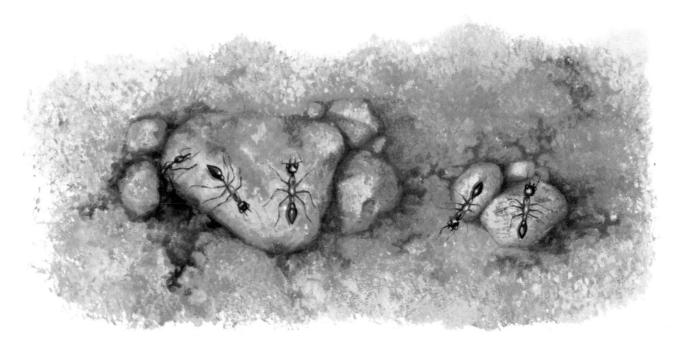

The giant petalura dragonfly of Queensland is the bulkiest dragonfly known, and one of the largest flying insects. It belongs to a group that was dominant and world-wide when dinosaurs roamed the Earth.

significance. Another of their primitive features is the failure of any worker to guide or call other workers to any rich source of food that it finds. This again is a habit very characteristic of the higher ants.

Evidently the activity, large size, and formidable armament of these primitive ants proved no match for all the complexities of organization that evolved among the ants of the other continents. They have survived as a dominant group in Australia simply because there is a smaller variety and number of higher ants present on the continent as a result of its ages-long isolation. There is a close analogy here with the helplessness of primitive human cultures against the advance of modern civilization.

Dragonflies are regarded, with good reason, as a primitive group of insects. Some are more primitive than others and by far the most archaic dragonflies now living are those included in the family Petaluridae, already referred to in Chapter 1. Of the nine species of this family known, four are Australian, and one of these, the western petalura, was discovered near Perth as recently as 1957. The giant petalura of Queensland is the world's largest dragonfly, in the sense of being the most bulky, though a few other more lightly built species have longer bodies or greater wing-span.

The habits of adult petaluras are very much like those of other dragonflies. For example, they feed by catching other insects on the wing; being large and strong they not infrequently prey on smaller kinds of dragonflies. Their larvae differ from those of the modern highly evolved species in being by no means wholly aquatic. Petalurid larvae live in marshy places and dig burrows which are filled with water for most of their depth but open on to wet moss or other vegetation above the water surface. Their habits are not well known; some appear to wait at the mouth of the burrow and catch insects that wander close enough while others probably come out and walk about in search of prey. One species is known to live for five or six years as a larva, and this long pre-adult life may feature in all the species.

Although the Neotropical rain forest is pre-eminent for the number and diversity of its butterflies, the most magnificent of all are those found in the rain forest of the Papuan subregion of the Australian region. These butterflies are the swallowtails of the genus *Ornithoptera*, the true "birdwings," for that is what ornithoptera means. Some of the large Oriental swallowtails are also called by the same English name. These include Raja Brooke's birdwing and the beautiful black-and-gold *Troides* species, but the Papuan Ornithopteras are in a class of their own. The males are large, splendid butterflies, having the wings patterned in velvety black and iridescent green, blue, yellow, or orange, two of these colours being combined in some of them. The females are totally different, always dark brown with white or yellowish spots and streaks; they are huge, much bigger than the males, some being easily the largest butterflies in the world.

The largest species of this genus is, in fact, Queen Alexandra's birdwing, described and named *Ornithoptera alexandrae* in honour of Edward VII's queen by Lord Rothschild in 1907. The male of *O. alexandrae* spans about eight inches and its rather long and narrow wings are streaked with black and brilliant blue and green, the colours changing in intensity with the direction from which the light falls on them. This type of coloration is known as "structural" because it is produced not by pigments but by minute surface corrugations or other features of the scales breaking up the light into different wave-lengths. The female is, by contrast, a sombre butterfly that often reaches 10 inches in wing-span and sometimes 11. Queen Alexandra's birdwing is not a widespread species and is restricted to south-eastern Papua. In a recently published monograph of Australian and Papuan butterflies it is described as "increasingly rare due to indiscriminate collecting on behalf of wealthy dealers and collectors and the cutting down of the forests thereby destroying the growth of its larval food plant." It is encouraging to note that most of the Papuan birdwings are now protected by law, but laws of this kind require the weight of public opinion behind them to be effective. Conservation of the forests in which the butterflies live is certainly the most urgent measure needed.

The most widely distributed member of the genus is the Priamus birdwing, which occurs in New Guinea, in islands both west and east of it, and in Australia as far south as northern New South Wales. The males are green or blue and black with golden-yellow bodies; the colour and pattern varies with different localities and the species is divided accordingly into a number of subspecies. The food of the birdwing larvae (and also of their Oriental counterparts already mentioned) consists of various poisonous species of creeper of the genus *Aristolochia*. The butterflies retain the poison in their body fluids and thereby gain protection from attack by birds and other enemies.

Another group of butterflies that has its headquarters in the Papuan subregion are the Jezebels, genus *Delias*, of which over a hundred species are known. Many of them have a restricted distribution on single islands or in localities at high elevations in the mountains and no doubt there are still species awaiting discovery. They extend into the Oriental region as far as India and China, but in far less diversity than in the Australian tropics, and a few are found in the temperate parts of southern Australia.

The Jezebels belong to the same family, the Pieridae, as the familiar whites and clouded yellows of the north temperate regions. The upper sides of their wings are usually black and white, while the under sides, especially of the hind-wings, are brightly and even luridly patterned with red, orange, and yellow, producing the appearance that has inspired the name Jezebel, or Painted Jezebel. When at rest these butterflies sit with the hind-wings overlapping and largely concealing the fore-wings, so that they are coloured for maximum conspicuousness in the resting position.

The Jezebels are, in fact, yet another group of poisonous

The imperial white butterfly is a member of the genus Delias, *most of the species of which live in New Guinea and tropical Asia. This one, however, is found in temperate eastern Australia. The luridly coloured underside of the wings advertises the fact that the butterfly is distasteful to birds.*

butterflies that advertize their inedibility by flaunting a distinctive uniform. Their caterpillars present the curious paradox of being voracious eaters of leaves and yet friends of the trees; practically all those whose food plant is known feed on mistletoes *(Loranthus)*, which are sap-sucking parasites that are often completely defoliated by the Delias larvae. These plants have poisonous sap and are most probably the source of the butterflies' inedible quality. The caterpillars feed crowded together, sometimes in webs of silk, and even pupate gregariously as well. This habit of living gregariously, or in crowds, is a common feature of caterpillars that are poisonous or nasty to eat.

The Satyridae, or browns, are a family of butterflies of worldwide distribution, represented in the north temperate regions by such species as the European meadow brown and the North American wood-nymphs. They illustrate very well the basic composition of the butterfly fauna of continental Australia. If the

The little elia brown butterfly (left) is confined to the hills and mountains of southern Tasmania. The caterpillars feed on sedge and the insect flies in marshy country and along the banks of streams. The southern Australian members of this family of butterflies, the Satyridae, form an isolated group of great interest.

region was isolated before the end of the Mesozoic era, its butterflies (as in the case of Madagascar) must all have come from across the sea, since true butterflies had not evolved at that time, but originated later on the great land masses from which Australia had broken away. The northern part of the Australian region has always been fairly easily accessible from the Oriental region for animals having the power of flight. The Satyrids of northern, tropical Australia show clear evidence of this; the evening brown butterfly, for example, belongs to a species with a very wide distribution from Australia through the Oriental region to tropical Africa, and the bush-browns *(Mycalesis)* and the dingy-ring *(Ypthima)* have similar distributions. The

The regent skipper (right) is one of the most remarkable of all Australian butterflies, because it forms a kind of evolutionary link between butterflies and moths. In the male a structure is present linking the fore- and hind-wings, which is characteristic of moths, but seen in no other butterflies.

108

Satyrids and other butterflies, such as *Ornithoptera*, that are peculiar to the Papuan subregion can be supposed to have evolved in isolation from Oriental ancestors.

In southern, temperate Australia we encounter a wholly different assemblage of Satyrids. Some of them superficially resemble such species as the wall and speckled wood butterflies of Britain and Europe, but their anatomy reveals that they are not really closely allied to them. There are, in fact, five distinct genera of southern Australian Satyrids that are entirely confined to this area. The species illustrated is found only in Tasmania. This butterfly belongs to a genus that has one species with two subspecies, known as the leprea brown and elia brown, that are found in southern Tasmania, and in the central and northern parts of the island respectively. They are quite unlike any other known butterfly.

In the present state of our knowledge we can only assume that these southern Australian butterflies arrived on the continent during a remote period when the Antarctic climate was much less severe and continental drift had not removed the other southern lands, that is, South America and southern Africa, so far from Australia and Antarctica as to preclude the occasional flight of butterflies between them. Evolution to their present form has taken place in the cooler, southern part of Australia.

One of the most remarkable Australian butterflies, and also peculiar to the continent, is the beautiful regent skipper of the Queensland and New South Wales seaboard. The skippers are not now regarded as being true butterflies, but are placed separately in a superfamily, the Hesperioidea. The propriety of regarding them as intermediate between butterflies and moths is doubtful, but it does gain some support from a remarkable feature found in the regent skipper. Most moths, but no butterflies, have a device by which the fore-wings and hind-wings are coupled together. This device rather curiously differs consistently in the male and female moth wherever it is found. In the regent skipper the wings of the male are coupled together in the same manner as that found in the majority of male moths, but the feature is completely absent in the female.

The moth butterfly is an unusually large member of the family comprising the blues and hairstreaks. It is chiefly notable for its life history, the early stages of which are passed inside the nests of weaver ants. The caterpillars are serious enemies of the ants as they feed on their larvae.

The moth butterfly is an aberrant member of the great family of blues, coppers, and hairstreaks, the Lycaenidae, and is found in tropical Australia and Southeast Asia; a closely allied species occurs in New Guinea. It is the largest of all Lycaenids, thick-bodied and with a wingspan of three inches, and in flight it looks very like a large, tawny moth. Its life history is strange and interesting. The eggs are laid on trees infested with weaver ants, where they hatch into larvae, or caterpillars. At some early stage in their growth the larvae enter or are carried into the ants' nests, where they complete their growth. Most ants' nests harbour other insects that are tolerated or liked by the ants and do little or no harm to their hosts. The caterpillar of the moth butterfly, however, is a predatory invader, for it feeds on the larvae of the ants and must consume large numbers of them before it reaches full size. Its skin has the form of a rounded carapace, or horny shield, under which the legs are concealed, so that the ants cannot attack it effectively; the pupa retains the last larval skin as a protection. When the butterfly emerges from the pupal case it is covered with a thick felt of loosely attached scales which are brown and grey on the body and white on the wings, and these clog the jaws and the feet of the ants when they try to attack it.

With its large size, prominent jaws, and vivid coloration the rainbow stag-beetle is one of the most striking and beautiful of all beetles. It is known only from the rain forest of northern Queensland, where it inhabits stumps and fallen trunks of one particular species of tree.

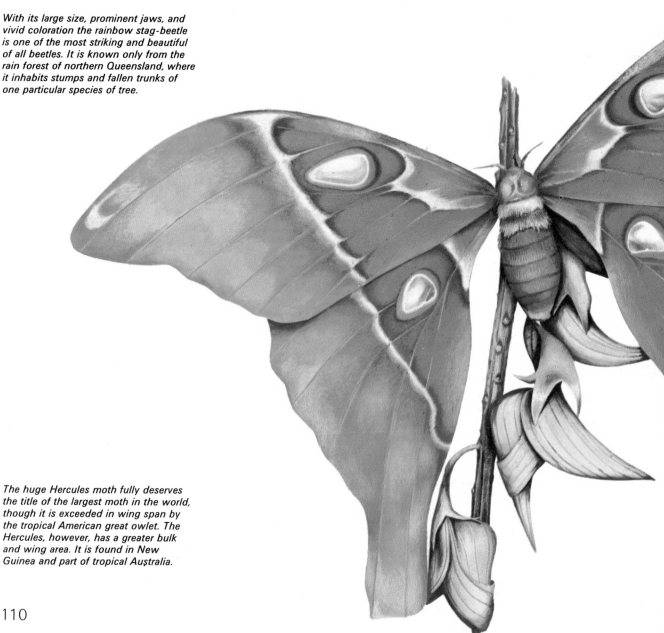

The huge Hercules moth fully deserves the title of the largest moth in the world, though it is exceeded in wing span by the tropical American great owlet. The Hercules, however, has a greater bulk and wing area. It is found in New Guinea and part of tropical Australia.

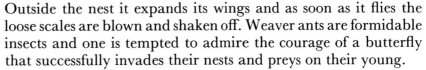

The swift-moths, or Hepialidae, form a group of very primitive moths that are found all over the world, but are most abundant in Australia. The bent-wing moth shown here is one of the finest and largest of them.

Outside the nest it expands its wings and as soon as it flies the loose scales are blown and shaken off. Weaver ants are formidable insects and one is tempted to admire the courage of a butterfly that successfully invades their nests and preys on their young.

We discussed the matter of the largest moth in Chapter 6, and mentioned the Hercules moth. This huge insect, found in the eastern Papuan subregion and the extreme north of Australia, is a Saturnid and a close relative of the Oriental Atlas moth, but the hind-wings are prolonged to form a pair of broad blunt tails, which add considerably to their area. This is a good example of a species that has evolved within the Australian region but whose ancestors were clearly Oriental. The wings of the female have a surface area of about 40 square inches and on this reckoning it is the largest of all the Lepidoptera.

The so-called "swift moths" (family Hepialidae) are among the most primitive moths existing today. An obvious archaic feature of them is seen in the pattern of the wing-veins, which is almost the same in fore- and hind-wings. In butterflies and all the other large moths the venation of the two pairs of wings is very different. The Hepialid moths are found in small numbers in all the zoogeographical regions but reach their greatest development in Australia. Of the total of about 200 species known, about 100 are Australian. They represent yet another relict element of the Australian fauna, a surviving sample of what were the dominant Lepidoptera in times perhaps as early as the Mesozoic era.

The bent-wing moth is one of the best known and largest of them. It is found in eastern New South Wales and its larvae live and feed by tunnelling in eucalyptus trees. The large white grub-like larvae of this and other Australian swift moths once formed quite an important part of the diet of the aborigines.

Before we leave the Australian region we must mention the resplendent rainbow stag beetle. This beetle is restricted to the rain forest of northern Queensland, where it inhabits logs and stumps of one particular species of tree. It is to be hoped that the Queensland rain forest will never be completely felled and cleared in the interests of agriculture and "development" for if this were to happen, this lovely insect would disappear forever.

8
Island
Insects

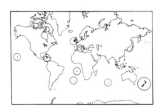

This chapter looks at some interesting insects of the British Isles, Corsica, Sardinia, Jamaica, New Zealand, St. Helena, the Galápagos Islands, Tristan da Cunha, and Hawaii.

Isolation is the mainspring of evolution, and the word isolation means, literally, segregation on an island. If some individuals of a population of any species become and remain separated from the rest, so that they breed only among themselves, the new population will slowly become different from the original one. If the separation is maintained long enough the new one will become so distinct that it can no longer interbreed with members of the original population, or at any rate cannot produce healthy and fertile offspring by such interbreeding. When this stage is reached a new species is well on its way to being formed.

The isolation can be brought about by changes of climate, resulting, perhaps, in a desert developing and dividing a fertile region into two areas, or by the slow uplift of a range of mountains, or even by changes in the habits of the animals concerned. We encountered a case of this when discussing the North American crickets. But the surest and probably the most frequent mode of isolation, leading to the formation of new species, is to become cut off or stranded on islands, and the majority of islands of any size provide examples of speciation in its various stages. Continent-sized islands like Australia and ancient South America conform to this rule, but we have dealt with them according to their status as zoogeographical realms.

During most of the Ice Age the British Isles formed continuous land with continental Europe. Ireland was separated from the mainland well before the end of the Ice Age, and a number of its insects have developed subspecies distinct from those found in Great Britain. The wood white and orange-tip butterflies are among these, and the Irish muslin moth differs from the British muslin moth in a peculiar way. In Britain the females are pure white with black dots, the males dark, sooty brown. Irish females

The largest and finest swallowtail butterfly of the New World is confined to a forested region of the island of Jamaica. This is Papilio homerus, *shown here sucking up moisture from a puddle. This superb butterfly could easily become extinct if its habitat were destroyed by development, and it is surely as well worth preserving as any other beautiful animal.*

are similar to British, but the males are pale ochre or white, differing but little from the females in appearance. The Irish muslin moth is regarded as a distinct subspecies.

The British swallowtail of East Anglia did not evolve as a consequence of the isolation of England by the formation of the Straits of Dover, which occurred only some 7,000 years ago. It is a relict of a much more widespread population that once lived in the great marshy area now occupied by the North Sea. Evolution generally takes longer than 7,000 years to produce subspecies, let alone full species.

Of course, the degree of speciation on an island depends on the remoteness in time of its isolation. Corsica and Sardinia in the Mediterranean Sea have been islands very much longer than Ireland, and some insects have evolved to form species confined to them. The most celebrated of these is the Corsican swallowtail (it is found on Sardinia too), which resembles the common swallowtail except that the hind-wing has a much shorter tail and is differently marked.

In the West Indies, Jamaica has a number of butterflies peculiar to its own territory, and among these is *Papilio homerus*, the largest and most magnificent swallowtail of the New World. It has a limited distribution within the island and is a precious insect that man should strive to protect from the extinction that would be likely to follow the "development" of its habitat.

Of all the world's large islands, those of New Zealand have by far the longest history of separation from any continental lands, and are the most remote from them. They are sometimes included in the Australian zoogeographical region, but do not really belong there and can almost be regarded as constituting a region of their own. New Zealand's extraordinary birds, its unique primitive reptile, the tuatara, and lack of native mammals (apart from bats and seals) are all well known. Its insects are less

In Great Britain the sexes of the muslin moth are very differently coloured, the male having sooty brown wings, while those of the female are white with black dots. In Ireland the females also have this appearance, but the males are white or cream-coloured and so do not differ greatly from the other sex. The Irish form is a distinct subspecies that has evolved due to the long isolation of Ireland. The lowest of the three figures is an Irish male.

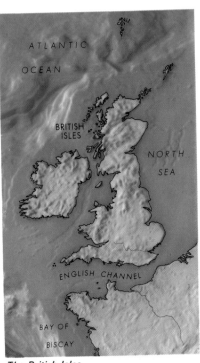

The British Isles.

114

Corsica and Sardinia.

The Corsican swallowtail, which is found also on Sardinia, is clearly related to the common swallowtail of continental Europe, but is sufficiently distinct to be regarded as a separate species. These two islands in the Mediterranean have been isolated from the mainland for much longer than Ireland, and so there has been time for the evolution on them of forms regarded as full species.

obviously distinctive, but the great majority of the native New Zealand insects are found nowhere else.

Of its small total, 11, of native and non-migrant butterflies the satyrids, or browns, are perhaps the most interesting. Their origin can be supposed to be the same as that of the southern Australian satyrids, a relict of a remote period when the southern continents were closer together and Antarctica enjoyed a temperate climate. This may seem a fantastic idea, but there is good geological evidence for it. Of the two New Zealand browns that we show here the beech forest butterfly is found on both islands, but the beautiful little tussock butterfly is a subalpine species confined to the South Island.

The wetas of New Zealand are a peculiar group of crickets, some very large, with four-inch long, heavy bodies. All of them are voiceless, lacking the stridulating apparatus on the wings that is characteristic of the cricket suborder; in most of them the wings are absent or vestigial. Some live on the forest floor and there is a cave-dwelling species with extremely long legs and antennae, giving it a total length of up to 14 inches.

Sometimes isolation leads to evolution of abnormally large forms; the giant monitor lizards of Komodo Island afford a well-known example of this. On the island of St. Helena in the Atlantic Ocean there lives a giant earwig. It is of the same genus as the common and widespread coastal earwig *Labidura riparia* and closely allied to it, but its size and some minor features of its anatomy justify regarding it as a distinct species. It was discovered in 1798, but lost sight of as a species until 1962, when a pair of the nippers, or forceps, were found buried in a sand dune. They were dry and brittle but not mineralized, and were 34 millimetres long. The original description of the St. Helena earwig was

AMSTERDAM
ISLAND
Flightless moth

GALÁPAGOS
ISLANDS
Striped sphinx
moth

CORSICA
& SARDINIA
Corsican swallowtail
butterfly

HAWAIIAN
ISLANDS
Lacewing flies
Nesomicromus va

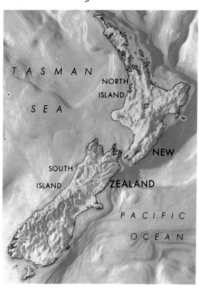

New Zealand.

© Geographical Projects

New Zealand has a longer history of isolation than any other of the world's large islands. As a consequence its animal life has evolved independently and most of the native New Zealand species are found there and nowhere else. Both the butterflies illustrated are quite unlike any others in the world. The one above is the beech forest butterfly, found in both North and South Islands. The lower one is the tussock butterfly, found in the South Island only, in a very different habitat. It is a subalpine species and lives in tussock grass country on the slopes of the mountains.

The insects known as wetas are peculiar to New Zealand, and a number of species are known, some of large size. Deinacrida heteracantha *(below) is one of these. The smaller species, on the right, is* Hemideina megacephala. *Wetas are allied to crickets.*

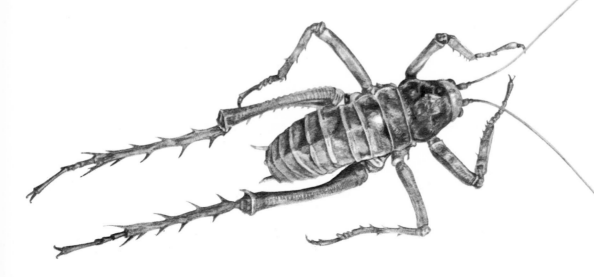

 *Pseudopsectra swezeyi*

 IRELAND Muslin moth

 NEW ZEALAND Beech forest butterfly

 Wetas *Hemideina megacephala*

 ST. HELENA Giant earwig

 Pseudopsectra cookeorum

 JAMAICA Butterfly *Papilio homerus*

 Tussock butterfly (South Island only)

 Deinacrida heteracantha

 TRISTAN DA CUNHA Wingless moth

 Strap winged fly

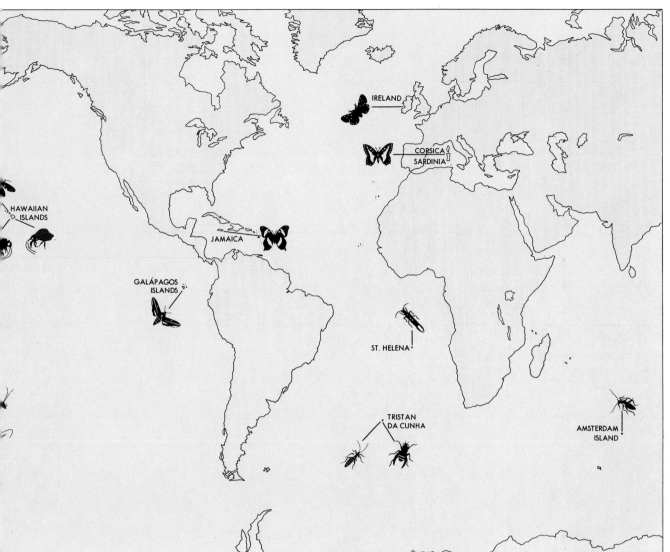

The giant earwig of St. Helena grows to 3 or 4 inches long and burrows under stones and in sand dunes. It is believed to be decreasing in numbers, but no reason is known for its decline.

overlooked and a new species was named to accommodate these enormous forceps.

In 1965 an expedition to the island rediscovered the living insect, most of the specimens being found under large boulders. The forceps of the largest of them were only 24 millimetres long, much smaller than the semi-fossil pair found in 1962. By calculation from the living specimens the owner of the 1962 forceps must have been about four inches in total length. The insect seems to be very localized now, in the north-east part of the island, and there are fears that it is dying out for some unknown reason.

The butterflies and moths of the Galápagos Islands belong,

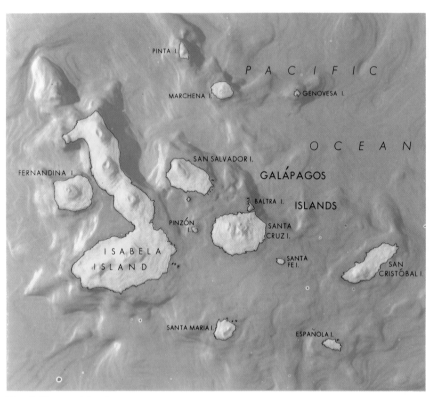

The Galápagos Islands.

On the Galápagos Islands there are several species of insects differing from their counterparts on the American mainland in their much smaller size. The striped sphinx moth is one of these, and we show a mainland and a Galápagos specimen both at actual size. This is probably a response to the climate of the islands, which is dry with occasional rather short periods of rain.

or are closely related, to species inhabiting the South American mainland, but most of them are conspicuously small in size. An example is the striped sphinx moth, of which we illustrate a specimen from the Islands, and one from the mainland. Giantism of the type illustrated by the earwig of St. Helena is not easy to explain, but local weather conditions probably account for the insect dwarfs of the Galápagos. A caterpillar can only grow just so fast; to reach a large size it needs to be able to feed continuously over a fairly long period. The climate of these islands is dry with occasional brief periods of rainfall. These promote a quick growth of leafy vegetation which soon withers and disappears. In these conditions natural selection will favour

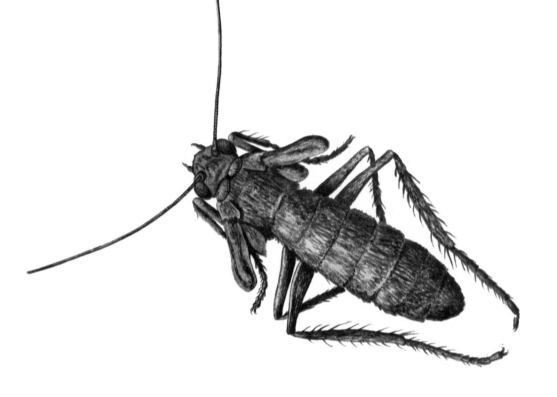

The strange-looking insect, shown here greatly enlarged, is a moth, by name Brachyapteragrotis patricei, *that lives on Amsterdam Island in the southern Indian Ocean. Its ancestors were winged, but a flying insect is in danger of being carried out to sea on windy, treeless islands. Natural selection therefore favoured the loss of wings and produced this almost wingless moth.*

caterpillars which complete their growth and pupate in a short time; but such caterpillars will be small and will develop into small moths and butterflies.

On small islands there is a tendency for insects whose continental relatives are fully capable of flight to have their wings reduced to vestiges and to confine themselves to crawling and hopping about on the ground. This phenomenon is very conspicuous on the widely scattered islands of the southern Atlantic and the oceanic waters that surround the Antarctic continent. On Tristan da Cunha only two out of 20 native insects have wings developed for flight and these flightless forms include moths and flies. The Kerguelen group of islands and Amsterdam Island to the north of them also harbour numbers of these curious flightless insects.

The islands of the far southern oceans are constantly swept by strong, cold winds, and they are devoid of trees, their natural vegetation being a tussocky grass. In these circumstances a

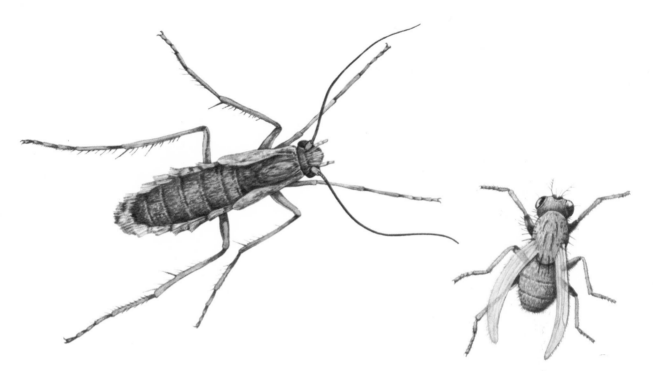

winged insect is in peril, as soon as it becomes airborne, of being blown away to sea and to practically certain death. The pressure of natural selection will operate strongly in favour of mutations in which the wings are stunted and ineffective for flight. By way of compensation the insects develop abnormal powers of running; a wingless moth found on one of these islands has been described as scuttling and hopping about with great activity.

It is a far cry from the cold desolation of the sub-Antarctic to the beautiful islands of Hawaii in the tropical Pacific Ocean. They were formed by volcanic action in rather recent geological times and their indigenous fauna consists of species that evolved in isolation, over a few millions of years, from the chance arrival of animals of quite modern types. Primitive creatures, such as inhabit New Zealand, are absent. It is difficult to imagine how the ancestors of the abundant and diverse Hawaiian plants and animals, including insects, ever reached these islands. Many must have been airborne, exhausted and lucky survivors of hurricanes which swept them away from their native lands. Others, perhaps even luckier, arrived on floating rafts of vegetation carried out of the mouths of flooding continental rivers and almost miraculously were stranded on the islands' shores. Insects must have arrived by both these hazardous avenues of immigration.

Among the Hawaiian insects we find again a number of flightless forms whose evolutionary ancestors were in all probability winged. Among the most curious of them are a group of lacewing flies, which on Hawaii occur in a variety of forms, from fully winged to wholly abnormal wingless species. One of these, *Pseudopsectra cookeorum*, has the fore-wings modified to form a rounded carapace rather like that of a beetle. Other normally winged insect orders, such as the flies (Diptera) also have flightless representatives in Hawaii.

The Hawaiian Islands are nothing like those of the bleak, windy Antarctic; they are warm, heavily forested (or were so

The Hawaiian Islands.

On the Hawaiian Islands a number of species of insects have become flightless for a less obvious reason than those on islands in the bleak and treeless southern oceans. An example of these is afforded by the lacewings (Neuroptera), of which three Hawaiian species are shown. Nesomicromus vagus, on the left, is a normal winged species. The centre figure is of Pseudopsectra swezeyi, whose wings are developed but useless for flight. In the remarkable Pseudopsectra cookeorum the wings have become fused to form a carapace something like that of a beetle. There are flightless flies also on Hawaii, and it is supposed that the absence of natural enemies, when these insects' ancestors arrived on the islands, led to disuse and degeneration of the wings.

in their pristine state) and in no way hazardous for an insect that can fly. Why, then, have the flightless forms evolved? We cannot be sure of the answer, but it seems likely that when the winged lacewings and flies arrived they found an environment with abundant food and few enemies. When wing abnormalities arose among them, by mutation, selective pressure was not strong enough to weed them out. The abnormal individuals survived and their abnormalities were inherited by their offspring, giving rise to species which would never have come into being in a harsher, more competitive environment. They became flightless not because it was advantageous to be so, but because there was no serious disadvantage in being unable to fly.

Now they are paying the penalty for their easy-going evolutionary past: ants, introduced from overseas by man, are exterminating them.

121

The Fossil History of Insects

Insects are not readily preserved as fossils and their evolutionary history in the geological record is far less complete than that of, say, the molluscs and the vertebrate animals, which have hard and durable shells or skeletons.

Nevertheless, enough fossil insects have been found in very fine-grained strata to give a good idea of how long ago most of the main groups originated and the stages they have passed through. Some of the groups, or orders, found as fossils have become extinct, but none of these were very different from the more primitive modern insects, and most of the existing orders originated quite early on in the fossil record. The most spectacular fossil insects are the giant dragonflies, whose remains are found in coal-bearing strata at Commentry in central France. The largest of them has a wing-span of 27 inches and they may be thought of as the dinosaurs of the insect world. But they lived 300 million years ago, 100 million years before the dinosaurs appeared on the Earth.

It is the wings of insects that are most frequently and perfectly preserved, as they lie flat and undistorted in fine-grained, thinly laminated strata. This is fortunate, as much of the evolutionary history of insects is recorded in the intricate patterns made by the chitinous supports or "veins" of the wings. These are often perfectly preserved in fossils, and our understanding of insect evolution is largely based on comparison of these fossil wings with living types.

The diagram on this page shows the geological periods from the beginning of the Devonian period, nearly 400 million years ago, to the present time. Periods earlier than the Devonian are not included because no fossils of insects have been found in strata older than this; before the Devonian both plant and animal life were almost confined to the seas and oceans. The Cenozoic, or Tertiary, era is subdivided into a number of comparatively short epochs, but details of these are not needed in a context of insect evolution, which was complete in its main outline by the beginning of the Cenozoic.

A brief summary of the evolution of the land vertebrates is given next to the table of periods, and the lines to the right of this indicate the age, as shown by fossil remains, of those existing insect orders of which fossils have been found.

The arrow is a reminder that the record is arranged, like the strata in a quarry or cliff face, with the older divisions below the younger, so that the passage of time runs upwards on the page. The figure at the base of each period represents the time, in millions of years ago, of its commencement, thus the Devonian period began about 395 million years ago and ended 345 million years ago. These figures convey little to the imagination, but an idea of the immensity of geological time can be conveyed by representing time on a scale of one yard to a thousand years. On this scale the time of Christ is six feet away: the beginning of the Devonian period is 225 *miles* away.

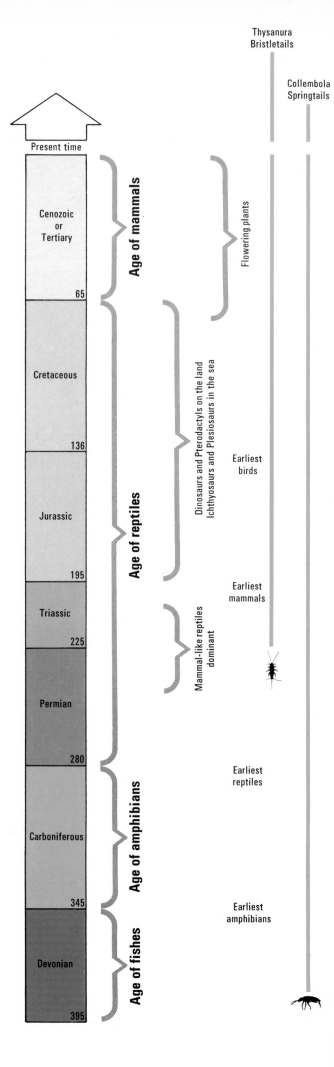

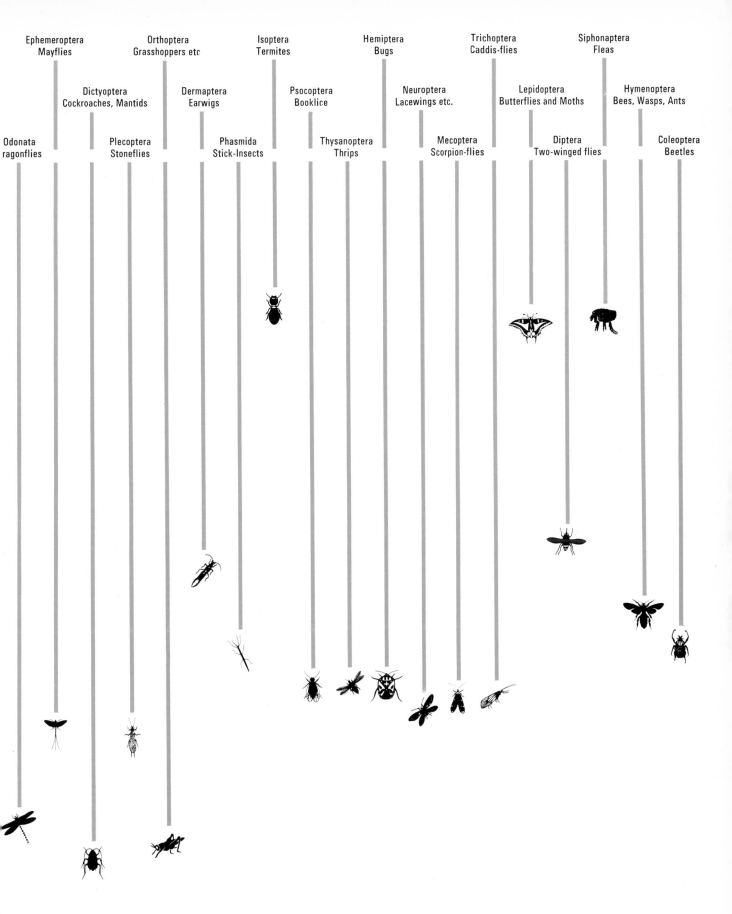

Ephemeroptera
Mayflies

Dictyoptera
Cockroaches, Mantids

Orthoptera
Grasshoppers etc

Dermaptera
Earwigs

Isoptera
Termites

Psocoptera
Booklice

Hemiptera
Bugs

Neuroptera
Lacewings etc.

Trichoptera
Caddis-flies

Lepidoptera
Butterflies and Moths

Siphonaptera
Fleas

Hymenoptera
Bees, Wasps, Ants

Odonata
ragonflies

Plecoptera
Stoneflies

Phasmida
Stick-Insects

Thysanoptera
Thrips

Mecoptera
Scorpion-flies

Diptera
Two-winged flies

Coleoptera
Beetles

123

Scientific Names

African eyed mantis	*Pseudocreobotra wahlbergi*
African giant swallowtail butterfly	*Papilio antimachus*
African migratory locust	*Locusta migratoria migratorioides*
African monarch butterfly	*Danaus chrysippus*
Alkali bee	*Nomia melanderi*
Alpine grizzled skipper	*Pyrgus andromeda*
American cockroach	*Periplaneta americana*
Apollo butterflies	Genus *Parnassius*
Arctic grayling butterfly	*Oeneis bore*
Argentine ant	*Iridomyrmex humilis*
Atlas moth	*Attacus atlas*
Bath white butterfly	*Pontia daplidice*
Bedstraw hawk-moth	*Celerio galii*
Beechey's bee	*Melipona beecheii*
Beech forest butterfly	*Dodonidia helmsii*
Bent-wing moth	*Zelotypia staceyi*
Blackflies	Genus *Simulium*
Black-mound termite	*Amitermes hastatus*
Branded imperial butterfly	*Eooxylides tharis*
British swallowtail butterfly	*Papilio machaon britannicus*
Bull's-eye moth	*Automeris io*
Camberwell beauty	*Nymphalis antiopa*
Clouded yellow butterfly	*Colias croceus*
Cockchafer	*Melolontha melolontha*
Colorado potato beetle	*Leptinotarsa decemlineata*
Common cockroach	*Blatta orientalis*
Compass termite	*Amitermes meridionalis*
Convolvulus hawk-moth	*Herse convolvuli*
Corsican swallowtail butterfly	*Papilio hospiton*
Cotton boll weevil	*Anthonomus grandis*
Desert locust	*Schistocerca gregaria*
Dewey ringlet	*Erebia pandrose*
Diadem butterfly	*Hypolimnas misippus*
Diana fritillary butterfly	*Speyeria diana*
Dwarf honeybee	*Apis florea*
Elia brown butterfly	*Nesoxenica leprea elia*
Eyed leaf insect	*Phyllium bioculatum*
Fall field-cricket	*Gryllus pennsylvanicus*
Fiddle beetles	Genus *Mormolyce*
Friar butterfly	*Amauris niavius*
Fruit-sucking moth	*Ophideres fullonica*
Giant honeybee	*Megapis dorsata*
Giant Malayan stick-insect	*Heteropteryx dilata*
Giant petalura dragonfly	*Petalura ingentissima*
Gipsy moth	*Lymantria dispar*
Goliath beetle	*Goliathus giganteus*
Great owlet moth	*Thysania agrippina*
Green lestes damselfly	*Lestes sponsa*
Harlequin bug	*Murgantia histrionica*
Hercules beetle	*Dynastes hercules*
Hercules moth	*Coscinoscera hercules*
House cricket	*Acheta domesticus*
Imperial white butterfly	*Delias harpalyce*
Indian leaf butterfly	*Kallima paracletes*
Io moth	*Automeris io*
Jamaican field-cricket	*Gryllus assimilis*
Japanese beetle	*Popilla japonica*
Kahan's sand beetle	*Lepidochora kahani*
Laboratory stick-insect	*Carausius morosus*
Large fungus-grower termite	*Macrotermes natalensis*
Leprea brown butterfly	*Nesoxenica leprea leprea*

Madagascar clubtail butterfly	*Atrophaneura antenor*
Maybug	*Melolontha melolontha*
Milkweed butterfly	*Danaus plexippus*
Mocker swallowtail butterfly	*Papilio dardanus*
Monarch butterfly	*Danaus plexippus*
Moth butterfly	*Liphyra brassolis*
Mountain ringlet butterflies	Genus *Erebia*
Mourning cloak butterfly	*Nymphalis antiopa*
Muslin moth	*Cycnia mendica*
Northern spring field-cricket	*Gryllus veletis*
Northern wood-cricket	*Gryllus vernalis*
Oak silk-moth	*Telea polyphemus*
Orange-tip butterfly	*Anthocharis cardamines*
Oriental flower mantis	*Hymenopus coronatus*
Painted lady butterfly	*Vanessa cardui*
Periodical cicada	The six species:
	Magicicada tredecim
	Magicicada tredecassini
	Magicicada tredecula
	Magicicada septendecim
	Magicicada cassini
	Magicicada septendecula
Plain tiger butterfly	*Danaus chrysippus*
Polyphemus moth	*Telea polyphemus*
Priamus birdwing butterfly	*Ornithoptera priamus*
Provence burnet moth	*Zygaena occitanica*
Rainbow stag beetle	*Phalacrognathus muelleri*
Raja Brooke's birdwing butterfly	*Trogonoptera brookiana*
Red admiral butterfly	*Vanessa atalanta*
Red locust	*Nomadacris septemfasciata*
Regent skipper butterfly	*Euschemon rafflesia*
Rhinoceros beetle	*Oryctes rhinoceros*
Robin moth	*Hyalophora cecropia*
Rocky Mountain locust	*Melanoplus spretus*
Ross's arctic tussock moth	*Gynaephora rossi*
Sacred scarab beetle	*Scarabaeus sacer*
St. Helena giant earwig	*Labidura herculeana*
Sand field-cricket	*Gryllus firmus*
Silverfish	*Lepisma saccharina*
Silver Y moth	*Plusia gamma*
Six-spot burnet moth	*Zygaena filipendulae*
Small Apollo butterfly	*Parnassius phoebus sacerdos*
South American palm weevil	*Rhynchophorus palmarum*
South-eastern field-cricket	*Gryllus rubens*
Southern wood-cricket	*Gryllus fultoni*
Spanish moon moth	*Graellsia isabellae*
Spruce budworm moth	*Choristoneura fumiferana*
Stilt-legged sand beetle	*Onymacris laeviceps*
Striped sphinx moth	*Deilephila lineata*
Swallowtail butterfly	*Papilio machaon*
Tobacco hornworm moth	*Protoparce quinquemaculatus*
Tomato hornworm moth	*Protoparce sexta*
Tussock butterfly	*Argyrophenga antipodum*
Vauthier's clouded yellow butterfly	*Colias vauthieri*
Weaver ant	*Oecophylla smaragdina*
Wetas	Genera:
	Deinacrida
	Hemideina
	Pachyrhamma and others
White-barred charaxes butterfly	*Charaxes brutus*
Wood white butterfly	*Leptidea sinapis*

Index

References in *italics* are to illustrations or captions to illustrations. References in **bold** are to map keys.

A

dragonflies (Odonata), fossil, *10–11*, 123; *see also* Petalurid family of dragonflies
dwarf honeybee, 56

earwigs (Dermaptera): fossil, 123; giant, of St Helena, 115, *117*, **117**, 118
Elia brown butterfly, **102–3**, *108*, 109
emperor (Saturniid) moths, 48–9, 56, 111; *see also* robin *and* Polyphemus moths
Ethiopian region, **14–15**, 18, 68–83
Europe, 17; maps, *30–1*, *34–5*; *see also* Palaearctic region
evening brown butterfly, 108
evolution: convergent, 30; importance of isolation in, 10, 12, 13, 112

fiddle beetle, **60–1**, 67, *67*
field-cricket, 40
fireflies (beetles), flashing signals of, *42–3*; *see also* Photinus, Photurus
fleas (Siphonaptera), fossil, 123
flight: effect of, on distribution, 16
flightless moth, **117**
fossil insects, *10–11*, 16, 100, 122–3
friar butterfly, mimicked by mocker swallowtail, *80*, 82
fruit-sucking moth, **60–1**, 66–7, *66*, 81
Fulgorid family of bugs, 97
fungi, cultivation of: by leaf-cutter ants, 94, *94*; by termites, 79
fungus-grower termites, **72–3**, *74–5*, **76–7**, *78–9*

G

Galápagos Islands: butterflies and moths of, 118–19; map, *118*
giant honeybee, 54, 56, **60–1**
giant Malayan stick-insect, **60–1**, 62
gipsy moth, 22, *24*, **26–7**, **34–5**, **44–5**, 48
glaciation, of Europe in Ice Age: map, *30–1*
glacier, locusts preserved in, 46
Goliath beetle, *68–9*, **72–3**, **76–7**, 79
Gondwana, former southern super-continent, *12*, 13, 17, 18
great owlet moth, *84–5*, **86–7**, 90, **92–3**
Grylloblatta, ancestor of crickets and cockroaches, *16*, 17
Grylloblattodea, 17

harlequin (cabbage) bug, **44–5**, 52, *53*
Hawaiian Islands: insects of, 120–1; map, *121*
hawk (sphinx) moths, 38, 49–50, 90; *see also* bedstraw *and* convolvulus hawk-moths, striped sphinx moth, *and* tobacco *and* tomato hornworms
head, thorax, and abdomen: body of insect divided into, 8
Heliconiid family of butterflies (poisonous), 89–90, *90*
Hepialid (swift) family of moths, 111, *111*
Hercules beetle, *68–9*, **86–7**, 91, *91*, **92–3**, 111
Hercules moth, 90, **102–3**, *110–11*
Hesperioidea, link between butterflies and moths, *108*, 109
Himalayas, *13*, 18
Holarctic region, **14–15**, 18
honeybee, 52, 54
honey-buzzard, 56
house cricket, 20, **26–7**, **34–5**, 39, *39*, **60–1**
Hymenoptera (bees, wasps, ants), 75; fossil, 123

Iberian peninsula, biological isolation of, 25, *29*
imperial white butterfly, **102–3**, *107*
India, origin of, *12*, 13, *13*
Indian leaf butterfly, *59*, **60–1**, 62
insects, 8; differentiated into main orders by Triassic times, 13, i.e. on Pangaea, 16; size of, limited by mode of breathing, 79–81; fossil, *10–11*, 16, 100, 122–3
Io ("bull's-eye") moth, 19, **44–5**, 51, *51*
Ireland, insects of, 112, 114
islands, insects of, 112–21; maps, **114–15**, *117*
Isoptera (termites), 75
Ithomiid family of butterflies (poisonous), 89, *90*

Jamaican field-cricket, **42**
Jamaican swallowtail butterfly, *88*, *112–13*, 114
Japanese beetle, **26–7**, **44–5**, *46*, 47–8, **60–1**
Jezebel (*Delias*) butterflies (poisonous), 107

Kerguelen Islands, wingless insects of, 119

L

laboratory stick-insect, 59, **60–1**
lacewing (Neuroptera), 121; fossil, 123; of Hawaii, **117**, 120, *121*
lantern fly, **86–7**, **92–3**, 97, *97*
Laurasia, former northern super-continent, *12*, 13, 17, 18
leaf-cutter ant, 79, **86–7**, **92–3**, 94, *94–5*
leaf-insects (butterflies), *54–5*, 59, *59*; in Africa, 81; *see also* Indian *and* ocellated leaf-insects
Lepidoptera (butterflies and moths), fossil, 123
leprea brown butterfly, **102–3**, 109
life-cycle of insects, in cold climates, 40
locusts: in United States, 43; *see also* African migratory, desert, red, *and* Rocky Mountain locusts
Lycaenid family of butterflies, 63, 110
Lycorea halia, Danaid butterfly, *90*

Madagascar: map, *81*; zoogeography of, 83
Madagascar endemic moth, **76–7**
Madagascar swallowtail (clubtail) butterfly (poisonous), **76–7**, *81*, 83
Malagasy sub-region, 83
Malay peninsula, zoogeography of, 56–9, *58*
mantises, 62; fossil, 123; *see also* African eyed *and* Oriental flower mantises
Mastotermes, 100–1, *100–1*, **102–3**
mating, attraction of opposite sex in: by flashes of light (fireflies), *42–3*; by scent (gipsy moth), 48; by song, (cicada) 42, (cricket) 40, 42
mayflies (Ephemeroptera), fossil, 123
meadow brown butterfly, 107
Mechanitis lysimnia, Ithomiid butterfly, *90*
Meganeura, giant dragonfly of Carboniferous period, *10–11*
Meliponid family of bees, 96–7
Mexico and Central America, map, *86–7*; *see also* Neotropical region
migration of insects, *21*, *37*, 37–9; maps, 21, *36*, *37*
mimicry: of face of cat or owl, *78*, 79, 89; of poisonous species, *47*, *63*, 63–5, *80*, 82, 89, *90*; of reptiles, 97; of snakes, 67
mocker swallowtail butterfly, **72–3**, **76–7**, *80*, 82–3

Artist Credits:

Anthony Swift 8 to 53, 69 to 83; Adrian Williams 55 to 67, 85 to 111 (except those shown below). The illustrations on pages 95(TR), 96, 99, and 100–101(T) were prepared by Richard Lewington/The Garden Studio.

Acknowledgments:

Page 63(B) after illustration on page 29 of Wolfgang Wickler, *Mimicry in Plants and Animals,* Weidenfeld and Nicolson Ltd., London, 1968. Page 88(T) after photograph on page 151 of Alexander B. Klots, *The World of Butterflies and Moths,* George G. Harrap and Co. Ltd., London 1958, © Horizons de France 1957, photograph Fachetti-Horizons de France. Page 111 after photograph on page 131 of Alexander B. Klots, *The World of Butterflies and Moths,* George G. Harrap and Co. Ltd., London 1958, © Horizons de France, 1957, photograph Fachetti-Horizons de France.

We should like to thank J. R. A. Gray B.Sc., Ph.D., Keeper of Invertebrate Zoology and E. G. Hancock B.Sc., A.M.A., of the City of Liverpool Museum, for their considerable help in supplying information and reference material for the illustrations.